# CARDINAL NEWMAN'S
# BEST PLAIN SERMONS

Edited by
VINCENT FERRER BLEHL, S.J.

Foreword by
MURIEL SPARK

HERDER AND HERDER

1964
HERDER AND HERDER NEW YORK
232 Madison Avenue, New York 16, N.Y.

Library of Congress Catalog Card Number: 64-19732
First published in Great Britain
© 1964 by Vincent Ferrer Blehl, S.J.
Foreword © 1964 by Muriel Spark
Printed in the United States of America

# CONTENTS

# FOREWORD

Over the past twelve years, at times when I have felt my mind becoming congested from hearing too many voices, including my own, I have turned to the sermons which Newman delivered to the undergraduates of Oxford when he was Vicar of St. Mary's. His voice from the pulpit was, by all accounts, something very special indeed. I am sure nothing has been lost in the past hundred and twenty years, only gained; for if there is one comprehensive thing that can be said about Newman's writings, it is that he has a 'voice'; it is his own and no one else's. To me, at least, it is a voice that never fails to start up, radioactive from the page, however musty the physical book.

If I can help it, I never read books for information only. I don't like books that are designed for spiritual improvement unless they are well written. I wouldn't touch the Bible if it wasn't interesting in historical, literary, and other ways beside its content. I read Newman's sermons because they are Newman's, not because they are sermons. He was as sincere as light. 'Every thought I think is thought, and every word I write is writing,' he said.

His reasoning is so pure that it is revolutionary in form. He does not go forward from point to point, he leads the mind inward, probing the secret places of the subject in hand. You can never anticipate, with Newman, what he is leading up to. Occupied entirely with the penetrable truths of his subject, he turns his argument with simple freedom, regardless of the moral direction it seems to be taking. He was out for the psychological penetration of moral character, and he achieved it.

I take as an example his sermon, 'Obedience without Love, as instanced in the Character of Balaam', because I think it shows not only his typical habits of thought and expression, but more noticeably than in any other sermon, the theme of the love of God which I think can be called Newman's basic one. It is, indeed, basic to the Christian religion that from the love of God all other movements of charity proceed. But Newman, who at an early age, conceived the thought 'of two and two only supreme and luminously self-evident beings, myself and my Creator', seems to me to have had an immediate relation to that one idea, the love of God, throughout his life and work.

This is the idea that he is directly investigating in the Sermon on Balaam. Balaam, he points out, is

> a high-principled, honourable, conscientious man. . . . He obeys as well as talks about religion; and this being the case, we shall feel more intimately the value of the following noble sentiments which he lets drop from time to time, and which, if he had shown less firmness in his conduct, might have passed for mere words, the words of a maker of speeches, a sophist, moralist, or orator. 'Let me die the death of the righteous, and let my last end be like his' . . .

It is not an ironic portrait. It is true there is a fine hair's-breadth of irony in the phrase '. . . the following noble sentiments which he lets drop from time to time', but that is by the way. It is Newman's manner always to praise the good in what he is bound to depart from. He goes on to elaborate and establish the delightful and noble aspects of Balaam, with as much sincerity as he employed in portraying the English Gentleman in his *Idea of a University*. And with as much sincerity, too, as he gave to the lovely outlines of his Oxford years in his *Apologia*. The *Apologia Pro Vita Sua* is the saddest love story in the world, it tells of his love for a beautiful idea of the spirit, the Anglican tradition in the setting of Oxford, and of his parting with this spiritual creature for the love of God. Balaam, he goes on to show, citing verse after verse in every perplexity of meaning, was a marvel of gracious, upright, pious living, lacking only the vital thing for the prosperity of his soul, the love of God. It was Newman's conviction that the nature of God was vastly misunderstood by his fellow countrymen when they assumed divine approval for the outward standards that they themselves approved. There was a moral movement in Newman's day, there is a moral outcry in our own times, there is worse to come: ethical, germ-free citizens will be springing up all over the place to prosper more and more visibly in public reward for their virtues. Newman declares:

> But if Scripture is to be our guide, it is quite plain that the most conscientious, religious, high-principled, honourable men (I use the words in their ordinary, not in their Scripture sense) may be on the side of evil, may be Satan's instruments in cursing, if that were possible, and at least in seducing and enfeebling the people of God.

Charles Kingsley's famous cry, 'What then does Dr. Newman mean?' was typical of the Christian moralists of the time. It is the doctrine of all Christians that without charity we are as sounding brass and a tinkling cymbal. But Newman points out some of the alarming implications of this nice poetry. What did he mean? He meant that God had not been educated at Rugby; that is more or less what he meant. Serious-minded people still call, from time to time, for a 'return to the moral standards of Christianity', by which they mean those codes of decency which have evolved in the chivalrous West from the Christian faith. Many hold that it is the morals that count, Christianity can go. I am not an expert in such matters, but I always sense, underlying these moralistic appeals and urges, a demand for something showy. Let us show the spirit of service, the people say, let us have some austerity, work harder, clean up our streets; morality must not only be done, it must be seen to be done; let us return to the hypocrisy of our forefathers— God used to like it so much when everyone went to church and didn't commit adultery.

Newman's contribution to this field of study is to say that conscientious people of high moral principle may be on the side of evil. He says that, however inspired, however honourable, they may be Satan's instruments in seducing and enfeebling the people of God. Moreover those who are genuinely pleasing in God's sight, only God knows. The disposition of every soul is a secret matter, not easily discernible.

I feel conscious of having very small excuse for putting down any observations at all as a foreword to a book comprising sermons by John Henry Newman, introduced as it is by such a fine and informed scholar as Father Vincent Ferrer Blehl. And why I have chosen to go off on a moralistic point, I really do not know; it seems a little redundant with a priest at hand. However, the pages are written now. My only claim to the subject is that of a novelist with a personal and literary debt to Newman. I spend most of my reading-time with Newman's books. I find every Life of Newman irresistible, even if it is the same story over and over again. When I am not reading Newman the books stand in peaceful reflection on the shelves, reading and revising themselves, so to speak, for the essays, lectures, sermons and letters all give out something new at each reading.

I have noticed that to those who have been attracted by Newman his personality continues very much alive. It is one of his gifts. He is far less dead, to me, than many of my contemporaries; and less dead, even, than Socrates for whom, in the day-dreams of my young youth, I thought it would be lovely to lay down my life. Socrates, too, had the love of God at heart; like him, Newman was said to be a 'corrupter of youth'. It was by way of Newman that I turned Roman Catholic. Not all the beheaded martyrs of Christendom, the ecstatic nuns of Europe, the five proofs of Aquinas, or the pamphlets of my Catholic acquaintance, provided anything like the answers that Newman did.

In his own time his persuasive power was greatly feared. But what did it consist of? Simplicity of intellect and speech. Simplicity is the most suspect of qualities; it upsets people a great deal. I think it was this, more than his actual doctrine, that caused suspicion to gather round the Vicar of St. Mary's. James Anthony Froude, an undergraduate at the time, has left one of the least ecstatic accounts of Newman's pulpit manner, and so I will quote him:

> I attended his church and heard him preach Sunday after Sunday; he is supposed to have been insidious, to have led his disciples on to conclusions to which he designed to bring them, while his purpose was carefully veiled. He was, on the contrary, the most transparent of men. He told us what he believed to be true. He did not know where it would carry him.

MURIEL SPARK

# INTRODUCTION

Muriel Spark, speaking of her reading for the year 1961, assigned first place to Newman's eight volumes of *Parochial and Plain Sermons*. Sermon reading has gone out of fashion; reading Newman's sermons has not. They are listened to as refectory reading by monks in France. Ecumenists find in them common ground. Written and preached when Newman was an Anglican, these sermons are so thoroughly Catholic that, long after his conversion to Catholicism, they were republished almost without correction. It is not surprising that the first volume, which appeared in 1834, 'put all other sermons out of the market', but their republication in 1868 the *Dublin Review* believed to be 'wholly without precedent'.[1] The sermons have since been reprinted many times, and critics such as Louis Bouyer believe that 'of all Newman's many writings, the *Parochial and Plain Sermons* will probably always be assigned the highest place'.[2]

The majority of these sermons were preached in St. Mary's Church, Oxford, from 1828, when Newman became its Vicar, to 1843, when he relinquished that office. A contemporary listener has given the following description of the church on a Sunday evening, as the congregation waited for Newman to begin his sermon:

> The great church, the congregation which barely filled it, all breathless with expectant attention. The gaslight, just

[1] *Dublin Review*, LXIV (April 1869), 309.

[2] Louis Bouyer, *Newman: His Life and Spirituality*, New York, 1960, p. 178.

at the left hand of the pulpit, lowered that the preacher might not be dazzled; themselves perhaps standing in the half-darkness under the gallery, and then the pause before those words in the 'Ventures of Faith' thrilled through them—'They say unto Him we are able.'[1]

Because it was both a parish church and the university church, the congregation was composed of local shop-keepers, tradesmen and college servants as well as bache-lors, junior masters and undergraduates. It was not the silvery quality of Newman's voice that accounted for the tremendous effect of these sermons, but the method and style in which they were written.

Newman's method was conditioned in part by the his-torical context. The situation was similar to that which Kierkegaard faced: unauthentic and formalistic Christian-ity. Newman described it in several sermons: 'Religion of the Day', for example, and 'The Religion of the Pharisee'. It was a religion which had so accommodated itself to the historical milieu that it substituted the refinement and en-lightenment of civilized society for the Kingdom of Christ. This worldly religion was not without solid values. It as-sured decency, order, respect, honesty, beautiful manners, and exquisite tact, but it was devoid of the supernatural, and could be lived without reference to Christ, grace, and the sacraments. Such a religion sedulously avoided the harsher and more difficult sides of the gospel message. It neither exacted nor effected any profound *metanoia*, because it substituted refined selfishness for genuine charity.

In opposition to this decadent Christianity Newman presented a fresh vision of scriptural truths. His vision is at once patristic and personal. The patristic quality one

[1] *Dublin Review*, LXIV (April 1869), 326.

senses in the sermons arises not from a patristic interpreta-
tion of this or that text of scripture. It stems rather from a
vital contact with and reflection upon the realities of which
the Bible speaks. For Newman and the Fathers, the Bible
presents the living drama of God's salvific relations with
men. The underlying direction in the movement of sacred
history is towards the coming of Christ, primarily in the
incarnation and secondarily at the end of the world. Funda-
mentally the sermons issued a call to holiness, which for
Newman, as for the Fathers, meant confrontation and conformity with Christ—the essence, the model and the motive
of sanctity.

> This is the very definition of a Christian—one who looks for
> Christ; not who looks for gain, or distinction, or power, or
> pleasure, or comfort . . . he surely is a . . . Christian, and he
> only who has no aim of this world . . . whose thoughts and aims
> have relations to the unseen, the future world.[1]

But if detachment from the world is the mark of the
Christian, so also the life of the Christian is one lived in the
presence of God. For him God is 'enthroned . . . at the very
springs of thought and affection'. The distinction between
the sincere and insincere Christian lies in this:

> that Christ dwells in the conscience of one, not of the other;
> that the one opens his heart to God, the other does not; the one
> views Almighty God only as an accidental guest, the other as
> Lord and owner of all that he is; the one admits Him as if for
> a night, or some stated season, the other gives himself over to
> God, and considers himself God's servant and instrument now
> and for ever.[2]

Newman's method of confronting men with Christ was
anchored in a deep and penetrating psychology of the

[1] *Sermons on Subjects of the Day*, pp. 278–9.

[2] *Parochial and Plain Sermons*, V, Sermon 16.

human mind of which the *Grammar of Assent* remains the definitive statement. There Newman distinguishes between 'real' and 'notional' knowledge. In the sermons he offers several descriptions of the process whereby abstract or 'notional' knowledge is converted into 'real'. Realization is, for example, 'to open one's heart to a truth'. A truth is assimilated when one responds to it, not with the intellect alone, but with one's entire being. Knowledge is then no longer abstract; it becomes an influential principle transforming conduct and opinion. Again, to realize a truth is to accept in one's life all the conclusions to which principles lead. Finally, realization means bringing facts into consciousness, contemplating them vividly, grasping them and bringing them home to oneself, so that their truth becomes a principle of action.

Newman's purpose in the sermons, then, was to lead men to realize vividly for themselves the mysteries of faith, to comprehend authentic Christianity as a concrete way of life, not merely as an abstract programme for living. Christian doctrine and morality were presented in a way that demanded an authentic response, a definite commitment of the entire being. To accomplish such a change in the consciousness of his hearers was no easy task. Mere logical reasoning would be ineffectual. Newman employed the more subtle method of implicit reasoning which was, in fact, a personal logic, a logic of conviction rather than of strict proof. By an accumulation of biblical examples, suggestions, analyses of attitudes of mind, Newman gradually brought his hearers to assimilate the meaning of Christian truths in relation to their personal lives. No longer could they ignore or reject Christian doctrine without a pang of conscience.

Newman's method of developing a sermon, therefore,

differs from that of other preachers. He does not proceed by logical steps from idea to idea, but keeps penetrating deeper and deeper into the same general idea until it becomes more concrete and personal. His thought over a wide area works downwards rather than sideways. Starting with the more universal aspect of his theme, he sees beneath it, the general; the specific beneath the general; and beneath all, the individual, and that the individual is Newman and his hearers. This is the explanation of the phenomenon noted by many of his contemporaries that Newman seemed to see into the very minds of his hearers and to be revealing to them their innermost thoughts. With keen psychological acumen he led them through a definite pattern of thought, which terminated in a changed attitude of mind. He analysed his audience's attitudes precisely in relation to the particular Christian attitude which he was trying to develop. In so doing he took account of the subtle variations of character and temperament, as well as the hidden deceptions and secret manoeuvres whereby men seek to escape from truth. He confronted them with their subtle self-deceptions, un-recognized pretensions, and spiritual insincerities, so that they might achieve an unconditioned willingness to be transformed by Christ. Religion, Newman insisted, becomes a vital and energizing force only when the individual is constantly aware of Christian dogmas, not as abstract truths, but as concrete realities. For in the Christian religion God reveals Himself as a Person, and demands a corresponding personal response. The Christian then must cultivate habits of personal religion; he must live continuously in the presence of God, and, by means of scriptural meditation, enter into a dialogue with Christ, which ever increases in depth. The sermons themselves provide an object lesson in such fruitful meditations. 'No one has ever touched the

Gospels with so much innate kinship of spirit as he,' says
W. Sanday, who believed that the minimum requirement
for writing a life of Christ would be the knowledge, the
profound faith and psychological penetration of a Newman.[1]
Finally, Newman's greatest achievement lay in the pro-
foundly difficult task of making the invisible world a real
one. In this he was successful.

> With his strong, easy, exact, elastic language, the instrument
> of a powerful and argumentative mind, he plunged into the
> deep realities of the inmost spiritual life, of which cultivated
> preachers had been shy. He preached so that he made you feel
> without doubt that it was the most real of worlds to him; he
> made you feel in time, in spite of yourself, that it was a real
> world with which you too had concern.[2]

Newman believed that one could become interested in
his sermons by reading the best of them. This anthology is
based upon that premise. It contains the sermons which
Newman mentioned in a letter to Ambrose St. John,
January 26, 1846, as being his best.[3]

In Sermon 1, Newman reminds Christians of their high
destiny:

> The perfect Christian state is that in which our duty and our
> pleasure are the same, when what is right and true is natural
> to us, and in which God's 'service is perfect freedom'. And this
> is the state towards which all true Christians are tending; it is
> the state in which the Angels stand; entire subjection to God
> in thought and deed is their happiness; an utter and absolute
> captivity of their will to His will, is their fullness of joy and
> everlasting life. But it is not so with the best of us, except in

[1] W. Sanday, 'Jesus Christ', *Dictionary of the Bible*, Ed. J. H. Hastings,
New York, 1902, II, 653.
[2] R. W. Church, *Occasional Papers*, London, 1897, II, 451.
[3] *The Letters and Diaries of John Henry Newman*, Ed. Charles Stephen
Dessain, London, Vol. XI, 1961, 98–99.

> part . . . we have a work, a conflict all through life. We have to
> master and bring under all we are, all we do, expelling all
> disorder and insubordination, and teaching and impressing on
> every part of us, of soul and body, its due place and duty, till
> we are wholly Christ's in will, affections, and reason, as we are
> by profession. . . .

But merely professed Christians fail in this persevering daily
discipline of self, which demands sustained effort, especially
in time of testing. In short, they wish to escape from the
bondage to perfection which ultimately is perfect freedom.
This sermon manifests the severity with which some critics
have charged the Preacher of St. Mary's. In reality Newman's severity is merely the clear recognition of the demands
of Christian perfection, not for the monk, the cleric or the
ascetic, but for the ordinary Christian by reason of his
baptism.

Newman would not let the ordinary Christian forget the
tremendous responsibility of his freedom, 'the destiny of
accountableness, the fate of being free, the inalienable pre-
rogative of choosing between life and death, the inevitable
prospect of heaven and hell' (*PPS*, IV, Sermon 4). He ruth-
lessly exposed the attempt to escape from the high demands of
genuine Christianity into the lush pastures of social respectability.

> We know what it is to have a stake in any venture of this world.
> We venture our property in plans which promise a return; in
> plans which we trust, which we have faith in. What have we
> ventured for Christ? . . . I really fear, when we come to examine,
> it will be found that there is nothing we resolve, nothing we do,
> nothing we do not do, nothing we avoid, nothing we choose,
> nothing we give up, nothing we pursue, which we should
> not resolve, and do, and not do, and avoid, and choose, and give
> up, and pursue, if Christ had not died, and heaven were not
> promised us. I really fear that most men called Christians,

whatever they may profess, whatever they may think they feel, whatever warmth and illumination and love they may claim as their own, yet would go on almost as they do, neither much better nor much worse, if they believed Christianity to be a fable. When young, they indulge their lusts, or at least pursue the world's vanities; as time goes on, they get into a fair way of business, or other mode of making money; then they marry and settle; and their interest coinciding with their duty, they seem to be, and think themselves, respectable and religious men; they grow attached to things as they are; they begin to have a zeal against vice and error; and they follow after peace with all men. Such conduct indeed, as far as it goes, is right and praiseworthy. Only I say, it has not necessarily any thing to do with religion at all. . . .'

Newman's exposé of mere respectability as a substitute for genuine spirituality is propaedeutic to his insistence upon the need for daily discipline, prayer and self-control over the period of a lifetime. Richard Church, who as a youth of twenty heard the sermon (No. 4) just quoted, proclaimed that the predominant character of Newman's sermons was 'a passionate and sustained earnestness after a high moral rule, seriously realized in conduct'.[1] Christian faith was not something merely to be believed; for Newman it was something to be lived.

In Sermon 2, a magnificent moral portrait of Balaam, Newman warns of the dangers of compromise between selfishness and obedience to God. Charity, as Sermon 3 insists, is the one thing needful for the destruction of self-love. Once the primacy of charity is secured, the Christian will venture all for Christ, as Sermon 4 indicates, and he will find at his disposal the weapons of the saints (Sermon 5). Sincerity with self, with God and with one's fellow men

[1] R. W. Church, *The Oxford Movement*, London, 3rd edition, 1892, p. 21.

R.–B

(Sermon 6) will characterize the speech and actions of the Christian. With personal gratitude to Christ (Sermon 7), he will seek God, who is secretly present (Sermon 8), and the ordinary actions of daily life will take on tremendous significance (Sermon 9), especially in the light of Christ's coming, a patristic theme which Newman develops with penetrating insight (Sermon 10). In the final three sermons (11, 12, and 13), Newman takes up several paradoxes involved in the Christian attitude of waiting for Christ's second coming. For example, otherworldliness never involves a neglect of one's commitments and duties in this life, as non-Christians have sometimes erroneously supposed. 'Nay, we may form large plans, we may busy ourselves in new undertakings, we may begin great works which we cannot do more than begin; we may make provision for the future, and anticipate in our acts the certainty of centuries to come, yet be looking out for Christ.' Neither does the fear of Christ's coming disturb the cheerfulness and equanimity of the Christian character; for

> It is as clear a duty to rejoice in the prospect of Christ's coming, as if we were not told to fear it. The duty of fearing does but perfect our joy; that joy alone is true Christian joy, which is informed and quickened by fear, and made thereby sober and reverent.
>
> How joy and fear can be reconciled, words cannot show. Act and deed alone can show how. Let a man try both to fear and to rejoice, as Christ and His Apostles tell him, and in time he will learn how; but when he has learned, he will be as little able to explain how it is he does both, as he was before. He will seem inconsistent, and may easily be proved to be so, to the satisfaction of irreligious men. . . . He becomes the paradox which Scripture enjoins. . . .
>
> May we learn to mature all graces in us—fear and trembling,

watching and repenting, because Christ is coming; joyful, thankful, and careless of the future, because He is come.

Above all the true Christian enjoys peace of mind, for 'God is the God of peace, and in giving us peace He does but give Himself, He does but manifest Himself to us; for His presence is peace'.

The text used in this anthology is that published by W. J. Copeland in 1868. It reproduces the text of the editions published when Newman was still a member of the Church of England, save that the spelling, capitalization, and punctuation have been brought into general conformity with modern British usage wherever possible. It is hoped that Protestants, Catholics and others may herein share the joy of reading Newman's sermons and that these selections will stimulate them to emulate Muriel Spark in reading and studying the entire eight volumes.

VINCENT FERRER BLEHL, S.J.

Fordham University
December 1962

*To*

*JOSEPH SLATTERY, S.J.*

*with*

*grateful appreciation*

# 1. IN THE SERVICE OF CHRIST

---

## THE STRICTNESS OF THE LAW OF CHRIST

*ROMANS VI. 18*
*'Being then made free from sin, ye became the servants of righteousness.'*

IN the passage of which these words form a part, St. Paul insists again and again on the great truth which they declare, that Christians are not their own, but bought with a price, and, as being so, are become the servants or rather the slaves of God and His righteousness; and this, upon their being rescued from the state of nature. The great Apostle is not content with speaking half the truth; he does not merely say that we are set free from guilt and misery, but he adds, that we have become the servants of Christ; nay, he uses a word which properly means *slaves*. Slaves are bought and sold; we were by nature slaves to sin and Satan; we are bought by the blood of Christ: we do not cease to be slaves. We no longer indeed belong to our old master; but a master we have, unless slaves on being bought become freemen. We are still slaves, but to a new master, and that master is Christ. He has not bought us, and then set us loose upon the world; but He has done for us what alone could complete His first benefit, bought us to be His servants or slaves. He has given us that only liberty which is really such, bond-service to Himself; lest if left to ourselves, we should fall back again, as we certainly should, to the cruel bondage

from which He redeemed us. But anyhow, whatever be the
consequences it involves, whatever the advantage, whatever
the trial, we did not cease to be slaves on being set free from
Satan; but we became subject to a new Master, to Him who
bought us.

This needs insisting on; for a number of persons who are
not unwilling to confess that they are slaves by nature, from
some cause or other have learned to think that they are not
bound to any real service at all, now that Christ has set
them free. Now if by the word *slavery*, some cruel and miserable state of suffering is meant, such as human masters
often inflict on their slaves, in that sense indeed Christians
are not slaves, and the word is improper to apply to them;
but if by being slaves, is meant that we cannot throw up our
service, change our place, and do as we will, in that sense it
is literally true, that we are more than servants to Christ,
we are, as the text really words it, slaves. Men often speak
as if the perfections of human happiness lay in our being
free to do or not to do, to choose and to reject. Now we are
indeed thus free, as far as this—that if we do not choose to
be Christ's servants, we can go back to that old bondage
from which He rescued us, and be slaves again to the
powers of evil. But though we are free to make our situation
worse, we are not free to be without service or post of any
kind. It is not in man's nature to be out of all service and to
be self-dependent. We may choose our master, but God or
mammon we must serve. We cannot possibly be in a neutral
or intermediate state. Such a state does not exist. If we will
not be Christ's servants, we are forthwith Satan's; and
Christ set us free from Satan only by making us His servants.
Satan's kingdom touches upon Christ's, the world touches
on the Church; and we cease to be Satan's property by
becoming Christ's. We cannot be without a master, such is

the law of our nature; yet a number of persons, as I have said, overlook it, and think their Christian liberty lies in being free from all law, even from the law of God. Such an error seems to have obtained even in St. Paul's time, and is noticed in the chapter before us. Men seem to have thought that, since the law of sin was annulled, and the terrors of the law of nature removed, that therefore they were under no law at all; that their own will was their law, and that faith stood instead of obedience. In opposition to this great mistake, St. Paul reminds his brethren in the text, that when they were 'made free from *sin*', they 'became the servants of *righteousness*'. And again, 'Sin shall not have dominion over you; for ye are not under the law', that is, the law of nature, 'but under grace', or (as he elsewhere expresses it), 'the law of faith', or, 'the law of the Spirit of life'. They were not without a master, but they had a gracious and bountiful one.

He says the same in other Epistles. For instance, 'He that is called, being free' (that is, free as regards this world), 'is Christ's servant' or slave. 'Ye are bought with a price: be not ye slaves of *men*', but, that is, be slaves of Christ. Again, after saying, 'Slaves, obey in all things your masters according to the flesh', he adds, 'for ye are slaves to the Lord Christ'. Elsewhere he speaks of himself as 'Paul a servant', or slave, as the word really means, 'of Jesus Christ'; and again, as 'not without law to God, but under the law to Christ'.[1]

Religion then is a necessary service; of course it is a privilege too, but it becomes more and more of a privilege, the more we exercise ourselves in it. The perfect Christian state is that in which our duty and our pleasure are the same, when what is right and true is natural to us, and in

---

[1] I Cor. vii. 22, 23; Col. iii. 22, 24; Rom. i. 1; I Cor. ix. 21.

which God's 'service is perfect freedom'. And this is the state towards which all true Christians are tending; it is the state in which the Angels stand; entire subjection to God in thought and deed is their happiness; an utter and absolute captivity of their will to His will, is their fullness of joy and everlasting life. But it is not so with the best of us, except in part. Upon our regeneration indeed, we have a seed of truth and holiness planted within us, a new law introduced into our nature; but still we have that old nature to subdue, 'the old man, which is corrupt according to the deceitful lusts'.[1] That is, we have a work, a conflict all through life. We have to master and bring under all we are, all we do, expelling all disorder and insubordination, and teaching and impressing on every part of us, of soul and body, its due place and duty, till we are wholly Christ's in will, affections, and reason, as we are by profession; in St. Paul's words, 'casting down imaginations and every high thing that exalteth itself against the knowledge of God, and bringing into captivity every thought to the obedience of Christ'.[2]

Now I may seem to have been saying what every one will at once confess. And yet, after all, nothing perhaps is so rare among those who profess to be Christians as an assent in practice to the doctrine that they are under a law; nothing so rare as strict obedience, unreserved submission to God's will, uniform conscientiousness in doing their duty—as a few instances will at once show.

Most Christians then will allow in general terms that they are under a law, but then they admit it with a reserve; they claim for themselves some dispensing power in their observance of the law. What I am saying is quite independent

[1] Eph. iv. 22.
[2] 2 Cor. x. 5.

of the question, what is the *standard* of obedience which each man proposes to himself? One man puts the line of his duty higher than another; some men take a low view of it, confining it to mere personal morality; others confine it to their social obligations; others limit it by some conventional law, which is received in particular classes or circles; others include religious observances. But whether men view the law of conscience as high or low, as broad or narrow, few indeed there are who make it a rule to themselves; few there are who make their own notion of it, whatever that be, binding on themselves; few who even profess to act up to it uniformly and consistently. Inquire of the multitude of men, as you meet them in the world, and you will find that one and all think it allowable at times to put themselves above the law, even according to their own standard of it; to make exceptions and reserves, as if they were absolute sovereigns of their conscience, and had a dispensing power upon occasions.

What is the sort of man whom the world accounts respectable and religious, in a high rank or a lower? At best he is such as this. He has a number of good points in his character; but some of these he has by nature, and if others have been acquired by trouble, it is either because outward circumstances compelled him to acquire them, or that he has from nature some active principle within him, of one kind or another, which has exerted itself, and brought other principles under, and rules him. He has acquired a certain self-command, because no one is respected without it. He has been forced into habits of diligence, punctuality, precision, and honesty. He is courteous and obliging; and has learned not to say all he thinks and feels, or to do all he wishes to do, on all occasions. The great mass of men of course are far from having in them so much that is really praiseworthy as this; but I am supposing the best. I am supposing then, that a man's character and station are such, that only now and then he will feel his inclinations or his interest to run counter to his duty. Such times constitute his trial; there is nothing to hinder him serving God in the ordinary course, but the proof of his sincerity lies in his conduct on these extraordinary occasions. Now this is the point to which I wish to draw attention; for these very occasions, which alone are his times of trial, are just the times on which he is apt to consider that he has a leave to dispense with the law. He dispenses with it at those very times when it is simply the law of God, without being also the law of self, and of the world. He does what is right, while the road of religion runs along the road of the world; when they part company awhile, he chooses the world, and calls his choice an exception. He does right for ninety-nine days, but on the hundredth he knowingly and wilfully does wrong; and if he does not justify, at least he absolves himself in doing it.

For instance; he *generally* comes to church, it is his *practice*; but some urgent business at a certain time presses on him, or some scheme of pleasure tempts him—he omits his attendance; he knows this is wrong, and says so, but it is only once in a way.

Again; he is strictly honest in his dealings; he speaks the truth, that is, it is his rule to do so; but if hard pressed, he allows himself now and then in a falsehood, particularly if it is a slight one. He knows he should not lie; he confesses it; but he thinks it cannot be helped; it is unavoidable from circumstances, as being his only way of escaping some great difficulty. In *such* a case it is, as he says, all fair, and so he gets over it; that is, in a case where he must either disobey God, or incur some temporal disadvantage.

Again; he has learned to curb his temper and his tongue; but on some unusual provocation they get the better of him. He becomes angry, says what he should not, perhaps curses and swears. Are not all men subject to be overtaken with anger or ill temper? That is not the point: the point is this—that he does not feel compunction afterwards, he does not feel he has done anything which needs forgiveness. On the contrary, he defends himself to himself, on the plea that such language is very *unusual* with him; he does not understand that he is under a law, which he may not put himself above, which he may not dispense with.

Once more; he is in general sober and temperate; but he joins a party of friends and makes merry; he is tempted to exceed. Next day he says that it is a long time since such a thing happened to him; it is not at all his way; he hardly touches wine or the like in common. He does not understand he has any sin to repent of, because it is but once in a way.

And now, I suppose, you quite understand what I mean, and I need not say more in explanation. Such men, being thus indulgent to themselves, are indulgent to each other; they make allowance for all around them, as taking what they give freely. This is the secret of being friends with the world, to have a sympathy and a share in its sins. They who are strict with themselves are strict with the world; but where men grant themselves a certain licence of disobedience, they do not draw the line very rigidly as regards others. Conscious of what might be said against themselves, they are cautious what they say against others; and they meet them on the understanding of a mutual sufferance. They learn to say that the private habits of their neighbours are nothing to them; and they hold intercourse with them only as public men, or members of society, or in the way of business, not at all as with responsible beings having immortal souls. They desire to see and know nothing but what is on the surface; and they call a man's personal history sacred, because it is sinful. In their eyes, their sole duty to their neighbour is, not to offend him; whatever his morals, whatever his creed, is nothing to them. Such are they in mature and advanced life; in youth, they are pliable as well as indulgent, they readily fall in with the ways of the world, as they come across them. They are, and have the praise of being, pleasant, good-tempered, and companionable. They are not bad-principled, or evilly disposed, or flagrantly irregular, but they are lax. They in no sense live by rule. They have high spirits, and all the natural amiableness which youth has to show, and they generally go right; but, since they have no root in themselves, an accident from within or without, the stirring of a passion, or the incitement of a friend, makes them swerve at once. They swerve, and they have little compunction afterwards; they forget it. They shrink from the notion of being under a law, and think religion gloomy as imposing it. They like their own way, and without any great extreme of sin, or at least any habits of sin, follow it. They are orderly and well-conducted, when among well-conducted people—at home, for instance; but they indulge themselves abroad, when temptation comes in their way. They have the world at will; they are free; alas! what a melancholy freedom! yet in one sense a freedom it is. A religious man must withdraw his eyes from sights which inflame his heart, recollecting our Saviour's caution; but a man of the world thinks it no harm to gaze where he should not, because he goes no further. A religious man watches his words; but the other utters whatever his heart prompts, and excuses himself for profane language, on the plea that he means nothing by it. A religious man will scruple about his society; but the other

takes part in jests and excesses, though he condemns while
he shares them, but not himself for sharing, and despises
those with whom he shares them. He can see life, as it is
called. He can go among all sorts of people, for he has no
troublesome ceremonial, no rule of religion to shackle him.
Perhaps he goes abroad, and then for a time he considers
himself to be in disguise, as an unknown person in unknown
countries, permitted to fall in with all things bad and good,
as they come. Or again, he may be so circumstanced, whatever his station, as to find himself engaged in what are
called politics; and then he thinks that though truth and
religion are certainly all-commanding and all-important,
yet still the world could not go on, public business would
be at a stand, political parties would be unable to act, all
that he really loves and reveres would become but of
secondary concern, if religion refused at all times to give
way ever so little. Again; a religious man carries his religion
into his conduct throughout the day; but lax persons will
do many things in private, which they would not like to be
known. They will overreach, if they can do it without
noise. They will break promises when made to an inferior.
Or, if they have time on their hands, they will be curious
and meddlesome; they will speak against others and spread
scandals. They will pry into things which do not concern
them, according to their station in life. They will listen
where they have no right to listen; they will read what they
have no right to read. Or they will allow themselves in
petty thefts, where they think they do no injury, excusing
themselves on the plea that what they take will never be
missed. Or in matters of trade, they think a certain sort and
degree of double-dealing allowable, and no dishonesty.
They argue with themselves as if it were not their business
to be true and just, but of others to find them out; and as if

fraud and cheating did not imply sin in the one party, but dullness in the other. If in humble life, they think it no harm to put on an appearance; to profess what is not strictly true, if they are to gain by it; to colour a story; or to affect to be more religious than they are; or to pretend to agree in religion with persons from whom they hope something; or to take up a religion if it is their interest to do so; or to profess two or three religions at once, when any alms or other benefit is to be given away.

These are a few out of a multitude of traits which mark an easy religion—the religion of the world; which would cast in its lot with Christian truth, were not that truth so very strict, and quarrels with it and its upholders, not as if it were not good and right, but because it is so unbending—because it will not suit itself to times and emergencies, and to the private and occasional likings and tastes of individuals. This is the kind of religion which St. Paul virtually warns us against, as often as he speaks of the Gospel as really being a law and a servitude. He indeed glories in its being such; for, as the happiness of all creatures lies in their performing their parts well, where God has placed them, so man's greatest good lies in obedience to God's law and in imitation of God's perfections. But the Apostle knew that the world would not think so, and therefore he insists on it. Therefore it is that he insists on the necessity of Christians '*fulfilling* the righteousness of the law'; fulfilling it, because till we aim at complete, unreserved obedience in all things, we are not really Christians at all. Hence St. James says, 'Whosoever shall keep the whole law, and yet offend in one point, he is guilty of all.' And our Saviour assures us that 'Whosoever shall break one of these least commandments, and shall teach men so, he shall be called least in the kingdom of heaven'; and that 'Except our righteousness shall exceed the righteousness of the Scribes and Pharisees', which was thus partial and circumscribed, 'we shall in no case enter into the kingdom of heaven'. And when the young man came to Him, saying that he had kept all the commandments, and asking what he lacked, He pointed out the 'one thing' wanting in him; and when he would not complete his obedience by that one thing, but went away sorrowful, then, as if all his obedience in other points availed him nothing, Christ added, 'Children, how hard is it for them that trust in riches to enter into the Kingdom of God?'[1] Let us not then deceive ourselves; what God demands of us is to fulfil His law, or at least to aim at fulfilling it; to be content with nothing short of perfect obedience—to attempt everything—to avail ourselves of the aids given us, and throw ourselves, not first, but afterwards on God's mercy for our shortcomings. This is, I know, at first hearing a startling doctrine; and so averse are our hearts to it that some men even attempt to maintain that it is an unchristian doctrine. A forlorn expedient indeed, with the Bible to refer to, and its statements about the strait gate and the narrow way. Still men would fain avail themselves of it, if they could; they argue that all enforcement of religion as a service or duty is erroneous, or what they call legal, and that no observance is right but what proceeds from impulse, or what they call the heart. They would fain prove that the law is not binding on us, because Christ has fulfilled it; or because, as is the case, faith would be accepted instead of obedience in those who had not yet had time to begin fulfilling it.

Such persons appeal to Scripture, and they must be refuted, as is not difficult, from Scripture; but the multitude of men do not take so much trouble about the matter.

[1] Rom. viii. 1–4; James ii. 10; Matt. v. 19, 20; Mark x. 21, 24.

Instead of even professing to discover what God has said, they take what they call a commonsense view of it. They maintain it is impossible that religion should really be so strict according to God's design. They condemn the notion as overstrained and morose. They profess to admire and take pleasure in religion as a whole, but think that it should not be needlessly pressed in details, or, as they express it, carried too far. They complain only of its particularity, if I may use the term, or its want of indulgence and consideration in little things; that is, in other words, they like religion before they have experience of it—in prospect—at a distance—*till* they have to be religious. They like to talk of it, they like to see men religious; they think it commendable and highly important; but directly religion comes home to them in real particulars of whatever kind, they like it not. It suffices them to have seen and praised it; they feel it a burden whenever they feel it at all, whenever it calls upon them to do what otherwise they would not do. In a word, the state of the multitude of men is this—their hearts are going the wrong way; and their real quarrel with religion, if they know themselves, is not that it is strict, or engrossing, or imperative, not that it goes too far, but that it *is* religion. It is religion itself which we all by nature dislike, not the excess merely. Nature tends towards the earth, and God is in heaven. If I want to travel north, and all the roads are cut to the east, of course I shall complain of the roads. I shall find nothing but obstacles; I shall have to surmount walls, and cross rivers, and go round about, and after all fail of my end. Such is the conduct of those who are not bold enough to give up a profession of religion, yet wish to serve the world. They try to reach Babylon by roads which run to Mount Sion. Do you not see that they necessarily must meet with thwartings, crossings, disappointments, and failure? They go mile after mile, watching in vain for the turrets of the city of Vanity, because they are on the wrong road; and, unwilling to own what they are really seeking, they find fault with the road as circuitous and wearisome. They accuse religion of interfering with what they consider their innocent pleasures and wishes. But religion is a bondage only to those who have not the heart to like it, who are not cast into its mould. Accordingly, in the verse before the text, St. Paul thanks God that his brethren had 'obeyed from the *heart* that *form* of teaching, into which they had been delivered'. We Christians are cast into a certain mould. So far as we keep within it, we are not sensible that it is a mould, or has an outline. It is when our hearts would overflow in some evil direction, then we discover that we are confined, and consider ourselves in prison. It is the law in our members warring against the law of the Spirit which brings us into a distressing bondage. Let us then see where we stand, and what we must do. Heaven cannot change; God is 'without variableness or shadow of turning'. His 'word endureth for ever in heaven', His law is from everlasting to everlasting. *We* must change. We must go over to the side of heaven. Never had a soul true happiness but in conformity to God, in obedience to His will. We must become what we are not; we must learn to love what we do not love, and practise ourselves in what is difficult. We must have the law of the Spirit of life written and set up in our hearts, 'that the righteousness of the law may be fulfilled in us', and that we may learn to please and to love God.

Lastly, as some men defend their want of strictness on what they consider the authority of Scripture, and others, that is, the majority, try to persuade themselves that religion cannot really be strict, whatever strong expressions or statements may be found in Scripture, others again there are, who take a more candid, but a more daring course. Instead of making excuses, such as I have been considering, they frankly admit the fact, and then go on to urge it as a valid argument against religion altogether. Instead of professing to like religion, *all but* its service, they boldly object that religion is altogether unnatural, and therefore cannot be incumbent on us. They say that it is very well for its ministers and teachers to set up a high doctrine, but that men are men, and the world is the world, and that life was not meant to be a burden, and that God sent us here for enjoyment, and that He will never punish us hereafter for following the law of our nature. I answer, doubtless this life was meant to be enjoyment; but why not a rejoicing in the Lord? We were meant to follow the law of our nature; but why of our old nature, why not of our new? Were we indeed in the state of our first nature, under the guilt and defilement of our birth-sin, then this argument might be urged speciously, though not conclusively of course then; but how does it apply to Christians? Now that God has opened the doors of our prison-house, and brought us into the kingdom of His Son, if men are still carnal men, and the world a sinful world, and the life of Angels a burden, and the law of our nature not the law of God, whose fault is it?

We Christians are indeed under the law as other men, but, as I have already said, it is the new law, the law of the Spirit of Christ. We are under grace. That law, which to nature is a grievous bondage, is to those who live under the power of God's presence, what it was meant to be, a rejoicing. When then we feel reluctant to serve God, when thoughts rise within us as if He were a hard Master, and that His promises are not attractive enough to balance the strictness of His commandments, let us recollect that we, as being Christians, are not in the flesh, but in the Spirit, and let us act upon the conviction of it. Let us go to Him for grace. Let us seek His face. Let us come where He gives grace. Let us come to the ordinances of grace, in which Christ gives His Holy Spirit, to enable us to do that which by nature we cannot do, and to be 'the servants of righteousness'. They who pray for His saving help to change their likings and dislikings, their tastes, their views, their wills, their hearts, do not indeed all at once gain what they seek—they do not gain it at once asking; they do not *perceive* they gain it while they gain it, but if they come continually day by day to Him, if they come humbly, if they come in faith—if they come, not as a trial how they shall like God's service, but throwing (as far as may be) their whole hearts and souls into their duty as a sacrifice to Him—if they come, not seeking a sign, but determined to go on seeking Him, honouring Him, serving Him, trusting Him, whether they see light, or feel comfort, or discern their growth, or no—such men *will* gain, though they know it not; they will find, even while they are still seeking; before they call, He will answer them, and they will in the end find themselves saved wondrously, to their surprise, how they know not, and when their crown seemed at a distance. 'They that wait on the Lord', says the Prophet, 'shall renew their strength; they shall mount up with wings as eagles; they shall run and not be weary, and they shall walk and not faint.'[1] *

[1] Isa. xl. 31.

* 'The Strictness of the Law of Christ', *PPS*, IV, Sermon 1.

# 2. THE DANGERS OF COMPROMISE

---

## OBEDIENCE WITHOUT LOVE, AS INSTANCED IN THE CHARACTER OF BALAAM

*NUMBERS XXII. 38*
'*The word that God putteth in my mouth, that shall I speak.*'

WHEN we consider the Old Testament as written by
divine inspiration, and preserved, beyond the time of
its own Dispensation, for us Christians—as acknowledged
and delivered over to us by Christ Himself, and pronounced
by St. Paul to be 'profitable for doctrine, reproof, correction, and instruction in righteousness'[1]—we ought not surely
to read any portion of it with indifference, nay, without
great and anxious interest. 'Lord, what wilt Thou have me
to do?' is the sort of inquiry which spontaneously arises in
the serious mind. Christ and His Apostle cannot have put
the Law and the Prophets into our hands for nothing. I
would this thought were more carefully weighed than it
commonly is. We profess indeed to revere the Old Testament; yet, for some reason or other, at least one considerable part of it, the historical, is regarded by the mass, even
of men who think about religion, as merely historical, as a
relation of facts, as antiquities; not in its divine characters,
not in its practical bearings, not in reference to themselves.
The notion that God speaks in it to them personally, the

[1] 2 Tim. iii. 16.

question, '*What* does He say?' 'What must I *do*?' does not occur to them. They consider that the Old Testament concerns them only as far as it can be made typical of one or two of the great Christian doctrines; they do not consider it in its fullness, and in its literal sense, as a collection of deep moral lessons, such as are not vouchsafed in the New, though St. Paul expressly says that it is 'profitable for instruction in righteousness'.

If the Old Testament history generally be intended as a permanent instruction to the Church, much more, one would think, must such prominent and remarkable passages in it as the history of Balaam. Yet I suspect a very great number of readers carry off little more from it than the impression of the miracle which occurs in it, the speaking of his ass. And not unfrequently they talk more lightly on the subject than is expedient. Yet I think some very solemn and startling lessons may be drawn from the history, some of which I shall now attempt to set before you.

What is it which the chapters in question present to us? The first and most general account of Balaam would be this—that he was a very eminent person in his age and country, that he was courted and gained by the enemies of Israel, and that he promoted a wicked cause in a very wicked way; that, when he could do nothing else for it, he counselled the Moabites to employ their women as means of seducing the chosen people into idolatry; and that he fell in battle in the war which ensued. These are the chief points, the prominent features of his history as viewed at a distance—and repulsive indeed they are. He took on him the office of a tempter, which is especially the Devil's office. But Satan himself does not seem so hateful near as at a distance; and when we look into Balaam's history closely, we shall find points of character which may well interest those who do not consider his beginning and his end. Let us then approach him more nearly, and forget for a moment the summary account of him, which I have just been giving.

Now first he was blessed with God's especial favour. You will ask at once, How could so bad a man be in God's favour? but I wish you to put aside reasonings, and contemplate facts. I say he was especially favoured by God; God has a store of favours in His treasure-house, and of various kinds—some for a time, some for ever—some implying His approbation, others not. He showers favours even on the bad. He makes His sun to rise on the unjust as well as on the just. He willeth not the death of a sinner. He is said to have loved the young ruler, whose heart, notwithstanding, was upon the world. His loving-mercy extends over all His works. How He separates in His own divine thought, kindness from approbation, time from eternity, what He does from what He foresees, we know not and need not inquire. At present He is loving to all men, as if He did not foresee that some are to be saints, others reprobates to all eternity. He dispenses His favours variously—gifts, graces, rewards, faculties, circumstances being indefinitely diversified, nor admitting of discrimination or numbering on our part. Balaam, I say, was in His favour; not indeed for his holiness' sake, not for ever; but in a certain sense, according to His inscrutable purpose—who chooses whom He will choose, and exalts whom He will exalt, without destroying man's secret responsibilities or His own governance, and the triumph of truth and holiness, and His own strict impartiality in the end. Balaam was favoured in an especial way above the mere heathen. Not only had he the grant of inspiration, and the knowledge of God's will, an insight into the truths of morality, clear and enlarged, such as even we Christians cannot surpass; but he was even admitted to conscious intercourse with God, such as we Christians have not. In our Sunday Services, you may recollect, we read the chapters which relate to this intercourse; and we do not read those which record the darker passages of his history. Now, do you not think that most persons, who know only so much of him as our Sunday lessons contain, form a very mild judgment about him? They see him indeed to be on the wrong side, but still view him as a prophet of God. Such a judgment is not incorrect as far as it goes; and I appeal to it, if it be what I think it is, as a testimony how highly Balaam was in God's favour.

But again, Balaam was, in the ordinary and commonly-received sense of the word, without straining its meaning at all, a very *conscientious* man. That this is so, will be plain from some parts of his conduct and some speeches of his, of which I proceed to remind you; and which will show also his enlightened and admirable view of moral and religious obligation. When Balak sent to him to call him to curse Israel, he did not make up his mind for himself, as many a man might do, or according to the suggestions of avarice and ambition. No, he brought the matter before God in prayer. He *prayed* before he did what he did, as a religious man ought to do. Next, when God forbade his going, he at once, as he ought, positively refused to go. 'Get you into your land,' he said, 'for the Lord refuseth to give me leave to go with you.' Balak sent again a more pressing message and more lucrative offers, and Balaam was even more decided than before. 'If Balak,' he said, 'would give me his house full of silver and gold, I cannot go beyond the word of the Lord my God, to do less or more.' Afterwards God gave him leave to go. 'If the men come to call thee, rise up, and go with them.'[1] Then, and not till then, he went.

[1] Num. xxii.

Almighty God added, 'Yet the word which I shall say unto thee, that shalt thou do.' Now, in the next place, observe how strictly he obeyed this command. When he first met Balak, he said, in the words of the text, 'Lo I am come unto thee; have I now any power at all to say anything? the word that God putteth in my mouth, that shall I speak.' Again, when he was about to prophesy, he said, 'Whatsoever He showeth me I will tell thee';[1] and he did so, in spite of Balak's disappointment and mortification to hear him bless Israel. When Balak showed his impatience, he only replied calmly, 'Must I not take heed to speak that which the Lord hath put in my mouth?' Again he prophesied, and again it was a blessing; again Balak was angered, and again the prophet firmly and serenely answered, 'Told not I thee, saying, All that the Lord speaketh, that I must do?' A third time he prophesied blessing; and now Balak's anger was kindled, and he smote his hands together, and bade him depart to his place. But Balaam was not thereby moved from his duty. 'The wrath of a king is as messengers of death.'[2] Balak might have instantly revenged himself upon the prophet; but Balaam, not satisfied with blessing Israel, proceeded, as a prophet should, to deliver himself of what remained of the prophetic burden, by foretelling more pointedly than before, destruction to Moab and the other enemies of the chosen people. He prefaced his prophecy with these unacceptable words—

Spake I not also unto thy messengers which thou sentest unto me, saying, If Balak would give me his house full of silver and gold, I cannot go beyond the commandment of the Lord, to do either good or bad of mine own mind? but what the Lord saith, that will I speak. And now behold, I go unto my people;

[1] Num. xxiii.
[2] Prov. xvi. 14.

come, therefore, and I will advertise thee what this people shall
do to thy people in the latter days.

After delivering his conscience, he 'rose up, and went and
returned to his place'.

All this surely expresses the conduct and the feelings of
a high-principled, honourable, conscientious man. Balaam,
I say, was certainly such, in that very sense in which we
commonly use those words. He said, and he did; he professed, and he acted according to his professions. There is no
inconsistency in word and deed. He obeys as well as talks
about religion; and this being the case, we shall feel more
intimately the value of the following noble sentiments which
he lets drop from time to time, and which, if he had shown
less firmness in his conduct, might have passed for mere
words, the words of a maker of speeches, a sophist, moralist,
or orator. 'Let me die the death of the righteous, and let my
last end be like his.' 'God is not a man that He should lie;
neither the son of man, that He should repent. . . . Behold, I have received commandment to bless; and He hath
blessed, and I cannot reverse it.' 'I shall see Him, but not
now; I shall behold Him, but not nigh.' It is remarkable
that these declarations are great and lofty in their mode of
expression; and the saying of his recorded by the prophet
Micah is of the same kind Balak asked what sacrifices were
acceptable to God. Balaam answered, 'He hath showed
thee, O man, what is good; and what doth the Lord require
of thee, but to do justly, and to love mercy, and to walk
humbly with thy God?'[1]

Viewing then the inspired notices concerning Balaam
in all their parts, we cannot deny to him the praise which,
if those notices have a plain meaning, they certainly do
convey that he was an honourable and religious man, with

[1] Micah vi. 3.

a great deal of what was great and noble about him; a man whom any one of us at first sight would have trusted, sought out in our difficulties, perhaps made the head of a party, and anyhow spoken of with great respect. We may indeed, if we please, say that he fell away afterwards from all this excellence: though, after all, there is something shocking in such a notion. Nay, it is not natural even that ordinarily honourable men should suddenly change; but however this *may* be said—it may be said he fell away; but, I presume, it *cannot* be said that he was other than a high-principled man (in the language of the world) *when* he so spoke and acted.

But now the strange thing is, that at this very time, *while* he so spoke and acted, he seems, as in one sense to be in God's favour, so in another and higher to be under His displeasure. If this be so, the supposition that he fell away will not be in point; the difficulty it proposes to solve will remain; for it will turn out that he was displeasing to God *amid* his many excellences. The passage I have in mind is this, as you will easily suppose. 'God's anger was kindled, because he went' with the princes of Moab, 'and the Angel of the Lord stood in the way for an adversary against him.' Afterwards, when God opened his eyes, 'he saw the Angel of the Lord standing in the way, and his sword drawn in his hand' . . . 'And Balaam said, I have *sinned*, for I knew not that thou stoodest in the way against me; now, therefore, if it displease thee, I will get me back again.' You observe Balaam said, 'I have sinned', *though* he avers he did not *know* that God was his adversary. What makes the whole transaction the more strange is this—that Almighty God had said before, 'If the men come to call thee, rise up, and go with them'; and that when Balaam offered to go back again, the Angel repeated, 'Go with the men.' And afterwards we find in the midst of his heathen enchantments

'God met Balaam', and 'put a word in his mouth'; and afterwards 'the Spirit of God came unto him'.

Summing up then what has been said, we seem, in Balaam's history, to have the following remarkable case, that is, remarkable according to our customary judgment of things: a man divinely favoured, visited, influenced, guided, protected, eminently honoured, illuminated—a man possessed of an enlightened sense of duty, and of moral and religious acquirements, educated, high-minded, conscientious, honourable, firm; and yet on the side of God's enemies, personally under God's displeasure, and in the end (if we go on to that) the direct instrument of Satan, and having his portion with the unbelievers. I do not think I have materially overstated any part of this description; but if it be correct only in substance, it certainly is most fearful, after allowing for incidental exaggeration—most fearful to every one of us, the more fearful the more we are conscious to ourselves in the main of purity of intention in what we do, and conscientious adherence to our sense of duty.

And now it is natural to ask, what is the *meaning* of this startling exhibition of God's ways? Is it really possible that a conscientious and religious man should be found among the enemies of God, nay, should be personally displeasing to Him, and that at the very time God was visiting him with extraordinary favour? What a mystery is this! Surely, if this be so, Revelation has added to our perplexities, not relieved them! What instruction, what profit, what correction, what doctrine is there in such portions of inspired Scripture?

In answering this difficulty, I observe in the first place that it certainly is impossible, quite impossible, that a really conscientious man should be displeasing to God; at the same time it is possible to be *generally* conscientious, or what the world calls honourable and high-principled, yet to be destitute of that religious fear and strictness, which God calls conscientiousness, but which the world calls superstition or narrowness of mind. And bearing this in mind, we shall, perhaps, have a solution of our perplexities concerning Balaam.

And here I would make a remark: that when a passage of Scripture, descriptive of God's dealings with man, is obscure or perplexing, it is as well to ask ourselves whether this may not be owing to some insensibility, in ourselves or in our age, to certain peculiarities of the Divine law or government therein involved. Thus, to those who do not understand the nature and history of religious truth, our Lord's assertion about sending a sword on earth is an obscurity. To those who consider sin a light evil, the doctrine of eternal punishment is a difficulty. In like manner the history of the flood, of the call of Abraham, of the plagues of Egypt, of the wandering in the desert, of the judgment on Korah, Dathan, and Abiram, and a multitude of other occurrences, may be insuperable difficulties, except to certain states and tempers of mind, to which, on the contrary, they will seem quite natural and obvious. I consider that the history of Balaam is a striking illustration of this remark. Those whose hearts, like Josiah's, are 'tender', scrupulous, sensitive in religious matters, will see with clearness and certainty what the real state of the case was as regards him; on the other hand, our difficulties about it, if we have them, are a presumption that the age we live in has not the key to a certain class of Divine providences, is deficient in a certain class of religious principles, ideas, and sensibilities. Let it be considered, then, whether the following remarks may not tend to lessen our perplexity.

Balaam obeyed God from a sense of its being right to do

so, but not from a *desire to please Him*, not from *fear and love*. He had other ends, aims, wishes of his own, distinct from God's will and purpose, and he would have effected these if he could. His endeavour was, not to please God, but to please self without displeasing God; to pursue his own ends *as far* as was consistent with his duty. In a word, he did not give his heart to God, but obeyed Him, as a man may obey human law, or observe the usages of society or his country, as something external to himself, because he knows he ought to do so, from a sort of rational good sense, a conviction of its propriety, expediency, or comfort, as the case may be.

You will observe he *wished* to go with Balak's messengers, only he felt he *ought not* to go; and the problem which he attempted to solve was *how* to go and yet not offend God. He was quite resolved he *would* anyhow act religiously and conscientiously; he was too honourable a man to break any of his engagements; if he had given his word, it was sacred; if he had duties, they were imperative: he had a character to maintain, and an inward sense of propriety to satisfy; but he would have given the world to have got rid of his duties; and the question was, *how* to do so without violence; and he did not care about walking on the very brink of transgression, so that he could keep from falling over. Accordingly he was not content with *ascertaining* God's will, but he attempted to *change* it. He inquired of Him a *second time*, and this was to tempt Him. Hence, while God bade him go, His anger was kindled against him because he went.

This surely is no uncommon character; rather, it is the common case even with the more respectable and praiseworthy portion of the community. I say plainly, and without fear of contradiction, though it is a serious thing to say, that the aim of most men esteemed conscientious and

religious, or who are what is called honourable, upright men,
is, to all appearance, not how to please God, but how to
please themselves without displeasing Him. I say confidently
—that is, if we may judge of men in general by what we
see—that they make this world the first object in their
minds, and use religion as a corrective, a restraint, upon
*too much* attachment to the world. They think that religion
is a negative thing, a sort of moderate love of the world, a
moderate luxury, a moderate avarice, a moderate ambition,
and a moderate selfishness. You see this in numberless ways.
You see it in the course of trade, of public life, of literature,
in all matters where men have objects to pursue. Nay, you
see it in religious exertions; of which it too commonly
happens that the chief aim is to attain *anyhow* a certain
definite end, religious indeed, but of man's own choosing;
not to please God, and *next*, if possible, to attain it; not to
attain it religiously, or not at all.

This surely is so plain that it is scarcely necessary to
enlarge upon it. Men do not take for the object towards
which they act, God's will, but certain maxims, rules, or
measures, right perhaps as far as they go, but defective
because they admit of being subjected to certain other
ultimate ends, which are not religious. Men are just,
honest, upright, trustworthy; but all this not from the love
and fear of God, but from a mere feeling of obligation to be
so, and in subjection to certain worldly objects. And thus
they are what is popularly called moral, without being
religious. Such was Balaam. He was in a popular sense a
strictly moral, honourable, conscientious man; that he was
not so in a heavenly and true sense is plain, if not from the
considerations here insisted on, at least from his after history, which (we may presume) brought to light his secret
defect, in whatever it consisted.

And here we see why he spoke so much and so vaunt-
ingly of his determination to follow God's direction. He
made a great *point* of following it; his end was not to please
God, but to keep straight with Him. He who loves does not
act from calculation or reasoning; he does not in his cool
moments reflect upon or talk of what he is doing, as if it
were a great sacrifice. Much less does he pride himself on
it; but this is what Balaam seems to have done.

I have been observing that his defect lay in this, that he
had not a single eye towards God's will, but was ruled by
other objects. But moreover, this evil heart of unbelief
showed itself in a peculiar way, to which it is necessary to
draw your attention, and to which I alluded just now in
saying that the difficulties of Scripture often arose from the
defective moral condition of our hearts.

*Why* did Almighty God give Balaam leave to go to
Balak, and then was angry with him for going? I suppose
for this reason, because his asking twice was tempting God.
God is a jealous God. Sinners as we are, nay as creatures of
His hands, we may not safely intrude upon Him, and make
free with Him. We may not dare to do that, which we should
not dare to do with an earthly superior, which we should be
punished, for instance, for attempting in the case of a king
or noble of this world. To rush into His presence, to address
Him familiarly, to urge Him, to strive to make our duty lie
in one direction when it lies in another, to handle rudely and
practise upon His holy word, to trifle with truth, to treat
conscience lightly, to take liberties (as it may be called) with
anything that is God's, all irreverence, profaneness, un-
scrupulousness, wantonness, is represented in Scripture not
only as a sin, but as felt, noticed, quickly returned on God's
part (if I may dare use such human words of the Almighty
and All-holy God, without transgressing the rule I am myself

laying down—but He vouchsafes in Scripture to represent Himself to us in that only way in which we can attain
to the knowledge of Him), I say all irreverence towards
God is represented as being jealously and instantly and
fearfully noticed and visited, as friend or stranger among
men might resent an insult shown him. This should be
carefully considered; we are apt to act towards God and the
things of God as towards a mere system, a law, a name, a
religion, a principle, not as against a Person, a living,
watchful, present, prompt and powerful Eye and Arm.
That all this is a great error, is plain to all who study
Scripture; as is sufficiently shown by the death of that
multitude of persons for looking into the ark—the death of
the Prophet by the lion, who was sent to Jeroboam from
Judah, and did not minutely obey the instructions given
him—the slaughter of the children at Bethel by the bears,
for mocking Elisha—the exclusion of Moses from the
promised land, for smiting the rock twice—and the judgment on Ananias and Sapphira. Now Balaam's fault seems
to have been of this nature. God told him distinctly not to
go to Balak. He was rash enough to ask a second time, and
God as a punishment gave him leave to ally himself with
His enemies, and to take part against His people. With this
presumptuousness and love of self in his innermost heart,
his prudence, firmness, wisdom, illumination, and general
conscientiousness, availed him nothing.

A number of reflections crowd upon the mind on the
review of this awful history, as I may well call it; and with
a brief notice of some of these I shall conclude.

1. First, we see how little we can depend, in judging of
right and wrong, on the apparent excellence and high
character of individuals. There *is* a right and a wrong in
matters of conduct, in spite of the world; but it is the

world's aim and Satan's aim to take our minds off from the
indelible distinctions of things, and to fix our thoughts upon
man, to make us the slaves of man, to make us dependent
on his opinion, his patronage, his honour, his smiles, and his
frowns. But if Scripture is to be our guide, it is quite plain
that the most conscientious, religious, high-principled,
honourable men (I use the words in their ordinary, not in
their Scripture sense), may be on the side of evil, may be
Satan's instruments in cursing, if that were possible, and at
least in seducing and enfeebling the people of God. For in
the world's judgment, even when most refined, a person is
conscientious and consistent, who acts up to his standard,
*whatever that is*, not he only who aims at taking the highest
standard. This is the world's highest flight; but in its ordinary judgment, a man is conscientious and consistent, who
is only inconsistent and goes against conscience in any
extremity, when hardly beset, and when he must cut the
knot or remain in present difficulties. That is, *he* is thought
to obey conscience, who only disobeys it when it is a praise
and merit to obey it. This, alas! is the way with some of the
most honourable of mere men of the world, nay of the mass
of (so-called) respectable men. They never tell untruths, or
break their word, or profane the Lord's day, or are dishonest
in trade, or falsify their principles, or insult religion, except
in very great straits or great emergencies, when driven into
a corner; and then perhaps they force themselves, as Saul
did when he offered sacrifice instead of Samuel—they force
themselves, and (as it were) undergo their sin as a sort of
unpleasant self-denial or penance, being ashamed of it all
the while, getting it over as quickly as they can, shutting
their eyes and leaping blindfold, and then forgetting it, as
something which is bitter to think about. And if memory is
ever roused and annoys them, they console themselves that

R.–D

after all they have only gone against their conscience now
and then. This is their view of themselves and of each other,
taken at advantage; and if anyone come across them who
has lived more out of the world than themselves, and has a
truer sense of right and wrong, and who fastens on some
one point in them, which to his mind is a token and warning
to himself against them, such a one seems, of course, narrow-
minded and overstrict in his notions. For instance; supposing some such man had fallen in with Balaam, and had
been privy to the history of his tempting God, it is clear that
Balaam's general correctness, his nobleness of demeanour,
and his enlightened view of duty, would not have availed
one jot or tittle to overcome such a man's repugnance to
him. He would have been startled and alarmed, and would
have kept at a distance, and in consequence he would have
been called by the world uncharitable and bigoted.

2. A second reflection which rises in the mind has relation to the wonderful secret providence of God, while all
things seem to go on according to the course of this world.
Balaam did not see the Angel, yet the Angel went out
against him as an adversary. He had no open denunciation
of God's wrath directed against him. He had sinned, and
nothing happened outwardly, but wrath was abroad and
in his path. *This* again is a very serious and awful thought.
God's arm is not shortened. What happened to Balaam is
as if it took place yesterday. God is what He ever was; we
sin as man has ever sinned. We sin without being aware of
it. God is our enemy without our being aware of it; and
when the blow falls, we turn our thoughts to the creature,
we illtreat our ass, we lay the blame on circumstances of
this world, instead of turning to Him. 'Lord, when Thy
hand is lifted up, they will not see; but they shall see', in the
next world if not here, 'and be ashamed for their envy at

the people; yea the fire of Thine enemies shall devour them'.[1]

3. Here too is a serious reflection, if we had time to pursue it, that when we have begun an evil course, we cannot retrace our steps. Balaam was forced to go with the men; he offered to draw back—he was not allowed—yet God's wrath followed him. This is what comes of committing ourselves to an evil line of conduct; and we see daily instances of it in our experience of life. Men get entangled, and are bound hand and foot in unadvisable courses. They make imprudent marriages or connexions; they place themselves in dangerous situations; they engage in unprofitable or harmful undertakings. Too often indeed they do not discern their evil plight; but when they do, they cannot draw back. God seems to say, 'Go with the men.' They are in bondage, and they must make the best of it; being the slave of the creature, without ceasing to be the responsible servants of God; under His displeasure, yet bound to act as if they could please Him. All this is very fearful.

4. Lastly, I will but say this in addition—God gives us warnings now and then, but does not repeat them. Balaam's sin consisted in not acting upon what was told him *once for all*. In like manner, you, my brethren, now hear what you may never hear again, and what perchance in its substance is the word of God. You may never hear it again, though with your outward ears you hear it a hundred times, because you may be impressed with it now, but never may again. You may be impressed with it now, and the impression may die away; and some time hence, if you ever think about it, you may then speak of it thus—that the view struck you at the time, but somehow the more you thought

[1] Isa. xxvi. 11.

about it, the less you liked or valued it. True; this *may* be so, and it *may* arise, as you think, from the doctrine I have been setting before you not being true and scriptural; but it *may* also arise from your having heard God's voice and not obeyed it. It may be that you have become blind, not the doctrine been disproved. Beware of trifling with your conscience. It is often said that second thoughts are best; so they are in matters of judgment, but not in matters of conscience. In matters of duty first thoughts are commonly best—they have more in them of the voice of God. May He give you grace so to hear what has been said, as you will wish to have heard, when life is over; to hear in a practical way, with a desire to profit by it, to learn God's will, and to do it! *

* 'Obedience without Love, As Instanced in the Character of Balaam', *PPS*, IV, Sermon 2.

# 3. THE PRIMACY OF CHARITY

## LOVE, THE ONE THING NEEDFUL

### (QUINQUAGESIMA)

*1 COR. XIII. 1*

'*Though I speak with the tongues of men and of angels, and have not charity, I am become as sounding brass, or a tinkling cymbal.*'

I SUPPOSE the greater number of persons who try to live Christian lives, and who observe themselves with any care, are dissatisfied with their own state on this point, viz. that, whatever their religious attainments may be, yet they feel that their motive is not the highest—that the love of God, and of man for His sake, is not their ruling principle. They may do much, nay, if it so happen, they may suffer much; but they have little reason to think that they love much, that they do and suffer for love's sake. I do not mean that they thus express themselves exactly, but that they are dissatisfied with themselves, and that when this dissatis-faction is examined into, it will be found ultimately to come to this, though they will give different accounts of it. They may call themselves cold, or hard-hearted, or fickle, or double-minded, or doubting, or dim-sighted, or weak in resolve, but they mean pretty much the same thing, that their affections do not rest on Almighty God as their great Object. And this will be found to be the complaint of religious men among ourselves, not less than others; their reason and their heart not going together; their reason tending heavenwards, and their heart earthwards.

I will now make some remarks on the defect I have described, as thinking that the careful consideration of it may serve as one step towards its removal.

Love, and love only, is the fulfilling of the Law, and they only are in God's favour in whom the righteousness of the Law is fulfilled. This we know full well; yet, alas! at the same time, we cannot deny that whatever good thing we have to show, whether activity, or patience, or faith, or fruitfulness in good works, love to God and man is not ours, or, at least, in very scanty measure; not at all proportionately to our apparent attainments. Now, to enlarge upon this.

In the first place, love clearly does not consist merely in great sacrifices. We can take no comfort to ourselves that we are God's own, merely on the ground of great deeds or great sufferings. The greatest sacrifices without love would be nothing worth, and that they are great does not necessarily prove they are done with love. St. Paul emphatically assures us that his acceptance with God did not stand in any of those high endowments, which strike us in him at first sight, and which, did we actually see him, doubtless would so much draw us to him. One of his highest gifts, for instance, was his spiritual knowledge. He shared, and felt the sinfulness and infirmities of human nature; he had a deep insight into the glories of God's grace, such as no natural man can have. He had an awful sense of the realities of heaven, and of the mysteries revealed. He could have answered ten thousand questions on theological subjects, on all those points about which the Church has disputed since his time, and which we now long to ask him. He was a man whom one could not come near without going away from

him wiser than one came: a fount of knowledge and wisdom ever full, ever approachable, ever flowing, from which all who came in faith gained a measure of the gifts which God had lodged in him. His presence inspired resolution, confidence, and zeal, as one who was the keeper of secrets, and the revealer of the whole counsel of God; and who, by look, and word, and deed encompassed, as it were, his brethren with God's mercies and judgments, spread abroad and reared aloft the divine system of doctrine and precept, and seated himself and them securely in the midst of it. Such was this great servant of Christ and Teacher of the Gentiles; yet he says, 'Though I speak with the tongues of men and of Angels, though I have the gift of prophecy, and understand all mysteries, and all knowledge, and have not charity, I am become as sounding brass, or a tinkling cymbal. . . . I am nothing.' Spiritual discernment, an insight into the Gospel covenant, is no evidence of love.

Another distinguishing mark of his character, as viewed in Scripture, is his faith, a prompt, decisive, simple assent to God's word, a deadness to motives of earth, a firm hold of the truths of the unseen world, and keenness in following them out; yet he says of his faith also, 'Though I have all faith, so that I could remove mountains, and have not charity, I am nothing.' Faith is no necessary evidence of love.

A tender consideration of the temporal wants of his brethren is another striking feature of his character, as it is a special characteristic of every true Christian; yet he says, 'Though I bestow all my goods to feed the poor, and have not charity, it profiteth me nothing.' Self-denying almsgiving is no necessary evidence of love.

Once more. He, if any man, had the spirit of a martyr; yet he implies that even martyrdom, viewed in itself, is no

passport into the heavenly kingdom. 'Though I give my
body to be burned, and have not charity, it profiteth me
nothing.' Martyrdom is no necessary evidence of love.

I do not say that at this day we have many specimens
or much opportunity of such high deeds and attainments;
but in our degree we certainly may follow St. Paul in them
—in spiritual discernment, in faith, in works of mercy, and
in confessorship. We may, we ought to follow him. Yet
though we do, still, it may be, we are not possessed of the
one thing needful, of the spirit of love, or in a very poor
measure; and this is what serious men feel in their own
case.

Let us leave these sublimer matters, and proceed to the
humbler and continual duties of daily life; and let us see
whether these too may not be performed with considerable
exactness, yet with deficient love. Surely they may; and
serious men complain of themselves here, even more than
when they are exercised on greater subjects. Our Lord says,
'If ye love Me, keep My commandments'; but they feel
that though they are, to a certain point, keeping God's
commandments, yet love is not proportionate, does not keep
pace, with their obedience; that obedience springs from
some source short of love. This they perceive; they feel
themselves to be hollow; a fair outside, without a spirit
within it.

I mean as follows: It is possible to obey, not from love
towards God and man, but from a sort of conscientiousness
short of love; from some notion of acting up to a *law*; that
is, more from the fear of God than from love of Him.
Surely this is what, in one shape or other, we see daily on
all sides of us; the case of men, living to the world, yet not
without a certain sense of religion, which acts as a restraint
on them. They pursue ends of this world, but not to the full;

they are checked, and go a certain way only, because they
dare not go further. This external restraint acts with
various degrees of strength on various persons. They all
live to this world, and act from the love of it; they all allow
their love of the world a certain range; but, at some
particular point, which is often quite arbitrary, this man
stops, and that man stops. Each stops at a different point
in the course of the world, and thinks everyone else profane
who goes further, and superstitious who does not go so far—
laughs at the latter, is shocked at the former. And hence
those few who are miserable enough to have rid themselves
of all scruples, look with great contempt on such of their
companions as have any, be those scruples more or less, as
being inconsistent and absurd. They scoff at the principle
of mere fear, as a capricious and fanciful principle; proceeding on no rule, and having no evidence of its authority,
no claim on our respect; as a weakness in our nature, rather
than an essential portion of that nature, viewed in its perfection and entireness. And this being all the notion which
their experience gives them of religion, as not knowing
really religious men, they think of religion only as a
principle which interferes with our enjoyments unintellig-
ibly and irrationally. Man is made to love. So far is plain.
They see that clearly and truly; but religion, as far as they
conceive of it, is a system destitute of objects of love; a
system of fear. It repels and forbids, and thus seems to
destroy the proper function of man, or, in other words, to
be unnatural. And it is true that this sort of fear of God, or
rather slavish dread, as it may more truly be called, *is* unnatural; but then it is not religion, which really consists,
not in the mere fear of God, but in His love; or if it be religion, it is but the religion of devils, who believe and
tremble; or of idolaters, whom devils have seduced, and

whose worship is superstition—the attempt to appease beings whom they love not; and, in a word, the religion of the children of this world, who would, if possible, serve God and Mammon, and, whereas religion consists of love *and* fear, give to God their fear, and to Mammon their love.

And what takes place so generally in the world at large, this, I say, serious men will feel as happening, in its degree, in their own case. They will understand that even strict obedience is no evidence of fervent love, and they will lament to perceive that they obey God far more than they love Him. They will recollect the instance of Balaam, who was even exemplary in his obedience, yet had not love; and the thought will come over them as a perplexity, what proof they have that they are not, after all, deceiving themselves, and thinking themselves religious when they are not. They will indeed be conscious to themselves of the sacrifice they make of their own wishes and pursuits to the will of God; but they are conscious also that they sacrifice them because they know they *ought* to do so, not simply from love of God. And they ask, almost in a kind of despair, How are we to learn, not merely to obey, but to love?

They say, How are we to fulfil St. Paul's words, 'The life which I now live in the flesh I live by the faith of the Son of God, who loved me, and gave Himself for me'? And this would seem an especial difficulty in the case of those who live among men, whose duties lie amid the engagements of this world's business, whose thoughts, affections, exertions, are directed towards things which they see, things present and temporal. In their case it seems to be a great thing, even if their *rule* of life is a heavenly one, if they *act* according to God's will; but how can they hope that heavenly Objects should fill their heart, when there is no room left for them? How shall things absent displace things present, things unseen the things that are visible? Thus they seem to be reduced, as if by a sort of necessity, to that state, which I just now described as the state of men of the world, that of having their hearts set on the world, and being only restrained outwardly by religious rules.

To proceed. Generally speaking, men will be able to bring against themselves positive charges of want of love, more unsatisfactory still. I suppose most men, or at least a great number of men, have to lament over their hardness of heart, which, when analysed, will be found to be nothing else but the absence of love. I mean that hardness which, for instance, makes us unable to repent as we wish. No repentance is truly such without love; it is love which gives it its efficacy in God's sight. Without love there may be remorse, regret, self-reproach, self-condemnation, but there is not saving penitence. There may be conviction of the reason, but not conversion of the heart. Now, I say, a great many men lament in themselves this want of love in repenting; they are hard-hearted; they are deeply conscious of their sins; they abhor them; and yet they can take as lively interest in what goes on around them as if they had no such consciousness; or they mourn this minute, and the next are quite impenetrable. Or, though, as they think and believe, they fear God's anger, and are full of confusion at themselves, yet they find (to their surprise, I may say) that they cannot abstain from any indulgence ever so trivial, which would be (as their reason tells them) a natural way of showing sorrow. They eat and drink with as good a heart as if they had no distress upon their minds; they find no difficulty in entering into any of the recreations or secular employments which come in their way. They sleep as soundly; and, in spite of their grief, perhaps find it most difficult to persuade themselves to rise early to pray for pardon. These are signs of want of love.

Or, again, without reference to the case of penitence, they have a general indisposition towards prayer and other exercises of devotion. They find it most difficult to get themselves to pray; most difficult, too, to rouse their minds to attend to their prayers. At very best they do but feel satisfaction in devotion *while* they are engaged in it. Then perhaps they find a real pleasure in it, and wonder they can ever find it irksome; yet if any chance throws them out of their habitual exercises, they find it most difficult to return to them. They do not like them well enough to seek them *from* liking them. They are kept in them by habit, by regularity in observing them; not by love. When the regular course is broken, there is no inward principle to act at once in repairing the mischief. In wounds of the body, nature works towards a recovery, and, left to itself, would recover; but we have no spiritual principle strong and healthy enough to set religious matters right in us when they have got disordered, and to supply for us the absence of rule and custom. Here, again, is obedience, more or less mechanical, or without love.

Again—a like absence of love is shown in our proneness to be taken up and engrossed with trifles. Why is it that we are so open to the power of excitement? Why is it that we are looking out for novelties? Why is it that we complain of want of variety in a religious life? Why that we cannot bear to go on in an ordinary round of duties year after year? Why is it that lowly duties, such as condescending to men of low estate, are distasteful and irksome? Why is it that we need powerful preaching, or interesting and touching books, in order to keep our thoughts and feelings on God? Why is it that our faith is so dispirited and weakened by hearing casual objections urged against the doctrine of Christ? Why is it that we are so impatient that objections should be answered? Why are we so afraid of worldly events, or the opinions of men? Why do we so dread their censure or ridicule?—Clearly because we are deficient in love. He who loves cares little for anything else. The world may go as it will; he sees and hears it not, for his thoughts are drawn another way; he is solicitous mainly to walk with God, and to be found with God; and is in perfect peace because he is stayed in Him.

And here we have an additional proof how weak our love is; viz. when we consider how little adequate our professed principles are found to be, to support us in affliction. I suppose it often happens to men to feel this, when some reverse or unexpected distress comes upon them. They indeed most especially will feel it, of course, who have let their words, nay their thoughts, much outrun their hearts; but numbers will feel it too, who have tried to make their reason and affections keep pace with each other. We are told of the righteous man, that 'he will not be afraid of any evil tidings, for his heart standeth fast, and believeth in the Lord. His heart is established, and will not shrink.'[1] Such must be the case of everyone who realizes his own words, when he talks of the shortness of life, the wearisomeness of the world, and the security of heaven. Yet how cold and dreary do all such topics prove, when a man comes into trouble? And why, except that he has been after all set upon things visible, not on God, while he has been speaking of things invisible? There has been much profession and little love.

These are some of the proofs which are continually brought home to us, if we attend to ourselves, of our want of love to God; and they will readily suggest others to us.

[1] Ps. cxii. 7, 8.

If I must, before concluding, remark upon the mode of overcoming the evil, I must say plainly this, that, fanciful though it may appear at first sight to say so, the comforts of life are the main cause of it; and, much as we may lament and struggle against it, till we learn to dispense with them in good measure, we shall not overcome it. Till we, in a certain sense, detach ourselves from our bodies, our minds will not be in a state to receive divine impressions, and to exert heavenly aspirations. A smooth and easy life, an uninterrupted enjoyment of the goods of Providence, full meals, soft raiment, well-furnished homes, the pleasures of sense, the feeling of security, the consciousness of wealth— these, and the like, if we are not careful, choke up all the avenues of the soul, through which the light and breath of heaven might come to us. A hard life is, alas! no certain method of becoming spiritually minded, but it is one out of the means by which Almighty God makes us so. We must, at least at seasons, defraud ourselves of nature, if we would not be defrauded of grace. If we attempt to force our minds into a loving and devotional temper, without this preparation, it is too plain what will follow—the grossness and coarseness, the affectation, the effeminacy, the unreality, the presumption, the hollowness (suffer me, my brethren, while I say plainly, but seriously, what I mean), in a word, what Scripture calls the Hypocrisy, which we see around us; that state of mind in which the reason, seeing what we should be, and the conscience enjoining it, and the heart being unequal to it, some or other pretence is set up, by way of compromise, that men may say, 'Peace, peace, when there is no peace.'

And next, after enjoining this habitual preparation of heart, let me bid you cherish, what otherwise it were shocking to attempt, a constant sense of the love of your Lord and

Saviour in dying on the cross for you. 'The love of Christ,' says the Apostle, 'constraineth us'; not that gratitude leads to love, where there is no sympathy, (for, as all know, we often reproach ourselves with not loving persons who yet have loved us), but where hearts are in their degree renewed after Christ's image, there, under His grace, gratitude to Him will increase our love of Him, and we shall rejoice in that goodness which has been so good to us. Here, again, self-discipline will be necessary. It makes the heart tender as well as reverent. Christ showed His love in deed, not in word, and you will be touched by the thought of His cross far more by bearing it after Him, than by glowing accounts of it. All the modes by which you bring it before you must be simple and severe; 'excellency of speech', or 'enticing words', to use St. Paul's language, is the worst way of any. Think of the Cross when you rise and when you lie down, when you go out and when you come in, when you eat and when you walk and when you converse, when you buy and when you sell, when you labour and when you rest, consecrating and sealing all your doings with this one mental action, the thought of the Crucified. Do not talk of it to others; be silent, like the penitent woman, who showed her love in deep subdued acts. She 'stood at His feet behind Him weeping, and began to wash His feet with tears, and did wipe them with the hairs of her head, and kissed His feet, and anointed them with the ointment'. And Christ said of her, 'Her sins, which are many, are forgiven her, for she loved much; but to whom little is forgiven, the same loveth little.'[1]

And, further, let us dwell often upon those His manifold mercies to us and to our brethren, which are the consequence of His coming upon earth; His adorable counsels, as

[1] Luke vii. 38, 47.

manifested in our personal election—how it is that we are called and others not; the wonders of His grace towards us, from our infancy until now; the gifts He has given us; the aid He has vouchsafed; the answers He has accorded to our prayers. And, further, let us, as far as we have the opportunity, meditate upon His dealings with His Church from age to age; on His faithfulness to His promises, and the mysterious mode of their fulfilment; how He has ever led His people forward safely and prosperously on the whole amid so many enemies; what unexpected events have worked His purposes; how evil has been changed into good; how His sacred truth has ever been preserved unimpaired; how Saints have been brought on to their perfection in the darkest times. And, further, let us muse over the deep gifts and powers lodged in the Church: what thoughts do His ordinances raise in the believing mind!—what wonder, what awe, what transport, when duly dwelt upon!

It is by such deeds and such thoughts that our services, our repentings, our prayers, our intercourse with men, will become instinct with the spirit of love. Then we do everything thankfully and joyfully, when we are temples of Christ, with His Image set up in us. Then it is that we mix with the world without loving it, for our affections are given to another. We can bear to look on the world's beauty, for we have no heart for it. We are not disturbed at its frowns, for we live not in its smiles. We rejoice in the House of Prayer, because He is there 'whom our soul loveth'. We can condescend to the poor and lowly, for they are the presence of Him who is Invisible. We are patient in bereavement, adversity, or pain, for they are Christ's tokens.

Thus let us enter the Forty Days of Lent now approaching. For Forty Days we seek after love by means of fasting. May we find it more and more, the older we grow, till death comes and gives us the sight of Him who is at once its Object and its Author.*

*'Love, the One Thing Needful', *PPS*, V, Sermon 23.

# 4. FULL COMMITMENT

## THE VENTURES OF FAITH

*MATT. XX. 22*
*'They say unto Him, We are able.'*

THESE words of the holy Apostles James and John
were in reply to a very solemn question addressed to
them by their Divine Master. They coveted, with a noble
ambition, though as yet unpractised in the highest wisdom,
untaught in the holiest truth—they coveted to sit beside
Him on His Throne of Glory. They would be content with
nothing short of that special gift which He had come to
grant to His elect, which He shortly after died to purchase
for them, and which He offers to us. They ask the gift of
eternal life; and He in answer told them, not that they
should have it (though for them it was really reserved),
but He reminded them what they *must venture for it*: 'Are
ye able to drink of the cup that I shall drink of, and to be
baptized with the baptism that I am baptized with? They
say unto Him, We are able.' Here then a great lesson is
impressed upon us, that our duty as Christians lies in this,
in making ventures for eternal life without the absolute
certainty of success.

Success and reward everlasting they will have, who persevere unto the end. Doubt we cannot that the ventures of
all Christ's servants must be returned to them at the Last
Day with abundant increase. This is a true saying—He

returns far more than we lend to Him, and without fail. But I am speaking of individuals, of ourselves one by one. No one among us knows for certain that he himself will persevere; yet every one among us, to give himself even a chance of success at all, must make a venture. As regards individuals, then, it is quite true that all of us must for certain make ventures for heaven, yet without the certainty of success through them. This, indeed, is the very meaning of the word 'venture'; for that is a strange venture which has nothing in it of fear, risk, danger, anxiety, uncertainty. Yes; so it certainly is; and in this consists the excellence and nobleness of *faith*; this is the very reason why *faith* is singled out from other graces, and honoured as the especial means of our justification, because its presence implies that we have the heart to make a venture.

St. Paul sufficiently sets this before us in the eleventh chapter of his Epistle to the Hebrews, which opens with a definition of faith, and after that gives us examples of it, as if to guard against any possibility of mistake. After quoting the text, 'The just shall live by faith', and thereby showing clearly that he is speaking of what he treats in his Epistle to the Romans as *justifying* faith, he continues, 'Now faith is the substance', that is, the realizing, 'of things hoped for, the evidence', that is, the ground of proof, 'of things not seen'. It is in its very essence the making present what is unseen; the acting upon the mere prospect of it, as if it really were possessed; the venturing upon it, the staking present ease, happiness, or other good, upon the chance of the future. And hence in another epistle he says pointedly, 'If in this life only we have hope in Christ, we are of all men most miserable.'[1] If the dead are not raised, we have indeed made a most signal miscalculation in the choice of life, and

[1] 1 Cor. xv. 19.

are altogether at fault. And what is true of the main doctrine itself is true also of our individual interest in it. This he shows us in his Epistle to the Hebrews, by the instance of the Ancient Saints, who thus risked their present happiness on the chance of future. Abraham 'went out, not knowing whither he went'. He and the rest died 'not having received the promises, but having seen them afar off, and were persuaded of them, and embraced them, and confessed that they were strangers and pilgrims on the earth.' Such was the faith of the Patriarchs: and in the text the youthful Apostles, with an untaught but generous simplicity, lay claim to the same. Little as they knew what they said in its fullness, yet their words were anyhow expressive of their hidden hearts, prophetic of their future conduct. They say unto Him, 'We are able.' They pledge themselves as if unawares, and are caught by One mightier than they, and, as it were, craftily made captive. But, in truth, their unsuspicious pledge was, after all, heartily made, though they knew not what they promised; and so was accepted. 'Are ye able to drink of My cup, and be baptized with My baptism? They say unto Him, We are able.' He in answer, without promising them heaven, graciously said, 'Ye *shall* drink indeed of My cup, and be baptized with the baptism that I am baptized with.'

Our Lord appears to act after the same manner towards St. Peter: He accepted his office of service, yet warned him how little he himself understood it. The zealous Apostle wished to follow his Lord at once: but He answered, 'Whither I go thou canst not follow Me now, but thou shalt follow me afterwards.'[1] At another time, He claimed the promise already made to Him; He said, 'Follow thou Me'; and at the same time explained it, 'Verily, verily, I say

[1] John xiii. 36.

unto thee, when thou wast young, thou girdedst thyself, and walkedst whither thou wouldest: but when thou shalt be old, thou shalt stretch forth thy hands, and another shall gird thee, and carry thee whither thou wouldest not.'[1]

Such were the ventures made in faith, and in uncertainty, by Apostles. Our Saviour, in a passage of St. Luke's Gospel, binds upon us all the necessity of deliberately doing the like —'Which of you, intending to build a tower, sitteth not down first and counteth the cost, whether he have sufficient to finish it? Lest haply, after he hath laid the foundation, and is not able to finish it, all that behold it, begin to mock him, saying, This man began to build, and is not able to finish.' And then He presently adds, 'So likewise, whosoever he be of you that forsaketh not all that he hath, he cannot be My disciple':[2] thus warning us of the full sacrifice we must make. We give up our all to Him; and He is to claim this or that, or grant us somewhat of it for a season, according to His good pleasure. On the other hand, the case of the rich young man, who went away sorrowful, when our Lord bade him give up his all and follow Him, is an instance of one who had *not* faith to make the venture of this world for the next, upon His word.

If then faith be the essence of a Christian life, and if it be what I have now described, it follows that our duty lies in risking upon Christ's word what we have, for what we have not; and doing so in a noble, generous way, not indeed rashly or lightly, still without knowing accurately what we are doing, not knowing either what we give up, nor again what we shall gain; uncertain about our reward, uncertain about our extent of sacrifice, in all respects leaning, waiting upon Him, trusting in Him to fulfil His promise, trusting in

[1] John xxi. 18–22.
[2] Luke xiv. 28–33.

Him to enable us to fulfil our own vows, and so in all respects proceeding without carefulness or anxiety about the future.

Now I dare say that what I have said as yet seems plain and unexceptionable to most of those who hear me; yet surely, when I proceed to draw the practical inference which immediately follows, there are those who in their secret hearts, if not in open avowal, will draw back. Men allow us Ministers of Christ to proceed in our preaching, while we confine ourselves to general truths, until they see that they themselves are implicated in them, and have to act upon them; and then they suddenly come to a stand; they collect themselves and draw back, and say, 'They do not see *this*— or do not admit *that*'—and though they are quite unable to say *why* that should not follow from what they already allow, which we show *must* follow, still they persist in saying, that they do not see that it does follow; and they look about for excuses, and they say we carry things too far, and that we are extravagant, and that we ought to limit and modify what we say, that we do not take into account times, and seasons, and the like. This is what they pretend; and well has it been said, 'Where there is a will there is a way'; for there is no truth, however overpoweringly clear, but men may escape from it by shutting their eyes; there is no duty, however urgent, but they may find ten thousand good reasons against it, in their own case. And they are sure to say we carry things too far, when we carry them home to themselves.

This sad infirmity of men, called Christians, is exemplified in the subject immediately before us. Who does not at once admit that faith consists in venturing on Christ's word without seeing? Yet in spite of this, may it not be seriously questioned whether men in general, even those of the better sort, venture anything upon His truth at all?

Consider for an instant. Let everyone who hears me ask himself the question, What stake has *he* in the truth of Christ's promise? How would he be a whit the worse off, supposing (which is impossible), but, supposing it to fail? We know what it is to have a stake in any venture of this world. We venture our property in plans which promise a return; in plans which we trust, which we have faith in. What have we ventured for Christ? What have we given to Him on a belief of His promise? The Apostle said that he and his brethren would be of all men most miserable if the dead were not raised. Can we in any degree apply this to ourselves? We think, perhaps, at present, we have some hope of heaven; well, *this* we should lose, of course; but after all, how should we be worse off as to our *present* condition? A trader, who has embarked some property in a speculation which fails, not only loses his prospect of gain, but somewhat of his own, which he ventured with the *hope* of the gain. This is the question, What have *we* ventured? I really fear, when we come to examine, it will be found that there is nothing we resolve, nothing we do, nothing we do not do, nothing we avoid, nothing we choose, nothing we give up, nothing we pursue, which we should not resolve, and do, and not do, and avoid, and choose, and give up, and pursue, if Christ had not died, and heaven were not promised us. I really fear that most men called Christians, whatever they may profess, whatever they may think they feel, whatever warmth and illumination and love they may claim as their own, yet would go on almost as they do, neither much better nor much worse, if they believed Christianity to be a fable. When young, they indulge their lusts, or at least pursue the world's vanities; as time goes on, they get into a fair way of business, or other mode of making money; then they marry and settle; and their interest coinciding with their duty, they seem to be, and think themselves, respectable and religious men; they grow attached to things as they are; they begin to have a zeal against vice and error; and they follow after peace with all men. Such conduct indeed, as far as it goes, is right and praiseworthy. Only I say, it has not necessarily anything to do with religion at all; there is nothing in it which is any proof of the presence of religious principle in those who adopt it; there is nothing they would not do still, though they had nothing to gain from it, except what they gain from it now: they do gain something now, they do gratify their present wishes, they are quiet and orderly, because it is their interest and taste to be so; but they *venture* nothing, they risk, they sacrifice, they abandon nothing on the faith of Christ's word.

For instance: St. Barnabas had a property in Cyprus; he gave it up for the poor of Christ. Here is an intelligible sacrifice. He did something he would not have done, unless the Gospel were true. It is plain, if the Gospel turned out a fable (which God forbid), but if so, he would have taken his line most unskilfully; he would be in a great mistake, and would have suffered a loss. He would be like a merchant whose vessels were wrecked, or whose correspondents had failed. Man has confidence in man, he trusts to the credit of his neighbour; but Christians do not risk largely upon their Saviour's word; and this is the one thing they have to do. Christ tells us Himself, 'Make to yourselves friends of the mammon of unrighteousness; that, when ye fail, they may receive you into everlasting habitations';[1] i.e. buy an interest in the next world with that wealth which this world uses unrighteously; feed the hungry,

[1] Luke xvi. 9.

clothe the naked, relieve the sick, and it shall turn to 'bags that wax not old, a treasure in the heavens that faileth not'.[1] Thus almsdeeds, I say, are an intelligible *venture*, and an evidence of faith.

So again the man who, when his prospects in the world are good, gives up the promise of wealth or of eminence, in order to be nearer Christ, to have a place in His temple, to have more opportunity for prayer and praise, he makes a sacrifice.

Or he who, from a noble striving after perfection, puts off the desire of worldly comforts, and is, like Daniel or St. Paul, in much labour and business, yet with a solitary heart, he too ventures something upon the certainty of the world to come.

Or he who, after falling into sin, repents in deed as well as in word; puts some yoke upon his shoulder; subjects himself to punishment; is severe upon his flesh; denies himself innocent pleasures; or puts himself to public shame—he too shows that his faith is the realizing of things hoped for, the warrant of things not seen.

Or again: he who only gets himself to pray against those things which the many seek after, and to embrace what the heart naturally shrinks from; he who, when God's will seems to tend towards worldly ill, while he deprecates it, yet prevails on himself to say heartily, 'Thy will be done'; he, even, is not without his sacrifice. Or he who, being in prospect of wealth, honestly prays God that he may never be rich; or he who is in prospect of station, and earnestly prays that he may never have it; or he who has friends or kindred, and acquiesces with an entire heart in their removal while it is yet doubtful, who can say, 'Take them away, if it be Thy will, to Thee I give them up, to Thee I

[1] Luke xii. 33.

commit them', who is willing to be taken at his word; he too risks somewhat, and is accepted.

Such a one is taken at his word, while he understands not, perhaps, what he says; but he is accepted, as meaning somewhat, and risking much. Generous hearts, like James and John, or Peter, often speak largely and confidently beforehand of what they will do for Christ, not insincerely, yet ignorantly; and for their sincerity's sake they are taken at their word as a reward, though they have yet to learn how serious that word is. 'They say unto Him, We are able'—and the vow is recorded in heaven. This is the case of all of us at many seasons. First, at Confirmation; when we promise what was promised for us at Baptism, yet without being able to understand how much we promise, but rather trusting to God gradually to reveal it, and to give us strength according to our day. So again they who enter Holy Orders promise they know not what, engage themselves they know not how deeply, debar themselves of the world's ways they know not how intimately, find perchance they must cut off from them the right hand, sacrifice the desire of their eyes and the stirring of their hearts at the foot of the Cross, while they thought, in their simplicity, they were but choosing the quiet easy life of 'plain men dwelling in tents'. And so again, in various ways, the circumstances of the times cause men at certain seasons to take this path or that, for religion's sake. They know not whither they are being carried; they see not the end of their course; they know no more than this, that it is right to do what they are now doing; and they hear a whisper within them, which assures them, as it did the two holy brothers, that whatever their present conduct involves in time to come, they shall, through God's grace, be equal to it. Those blessed Apostles said, 'We are able'; and in truth they were enabled to do and suffer as they had said. St. James was given strength to be steadfast unto death, the death of martyrdom; being slain with the sword in Jerusalem. St. John, his brother, had still more to bear, dying last of the Apostles, as St. James first. He had to bear bereavement, first, of his brother, then of the other Apostles. He had to bear a length of years in loneliness, exile, and weakness. He had to experience the dreariness of being solitary, when those whom he loved had been summoned away. He had to live in his own thoughts, without familiar friend, with those only about him who belonged to a younger generation. Of him were demanded by his gracious Lord, as pledges of his faith, all his eye loved and his heart held converse with. He was as a man moving his goods into a far country, who at intervals and by portions sends them before him, till his present abode is wellnigh unfurnished. He sent forward his friends on their journey, while he stayed himself behind, that there might be those in heaven to have thoughts of him, to look out for him, and receive him when his Lord should call. He sent before him, also, other still more voluntary pledges and ventures of his faith—a self-denying walk, a zealous maintenance of the truth, fasting and prayers, labours of love, a virgin life, buffetings from the heathen, persecution, and banishment. Well might so great a Saint say, at the end of his days, 'Come, Lord Jesus!' as those who are weary of the night, and wait for the morning. All his thoughts, all his contemplations, desires, and hopes, were stored in the invisible world; and death, when it came, brought back to him the sight of what he had worshipped, what he had loved, what he had held intercourse with, in years long passed away. Then, when again brought into the presence of what he had lost, how would remembrance revive, and familiar thoughts long buried come to life? Who shall dare to describe the blessedness of those who find all their pledges safe returned to them, all their ventures abundantly and beyond measure satisfied?

Alas! that we, my brethren, have not more of this high and unearthly spirit! How is it that we are so contented with things as they are—that we are so willing to be let alone, and to enjoy this life—that we make such excuses, if anyone presses on us the necessity of something higher, the duty of bearing the Cross, if we would earn the Crown, of the Lord Jesus Christ?

I repeat it; what are our ventures and risks upon the truth of His word? For He says expressly, 'Every one that hath forsaken houses, or brethren, or sisters, or father, or mother, or wife, or children, or lands, for My Name's sake, shall receive an hundredfold, and shall inherit everlasting life. But many that are first shall be last; and the last shall be first.'[1]*

[1] Matt. xix. 29, 30.

*'The Ventures of Faith', *PPS*, IV, Sermon 20.

# 5. THE WEAPONS OF SANCTITY

---

## THE WEAPONS OF SAINTS
### (WHITSUNTIDE)

*MATT. XIX. 30*
*'Many that are first shall be last, and the last shall be first.'*

THESE words are fulfilled under the Gospel in many ways. Our Saviour in one place applies them to the rejection of the Jews and the calling of the Gentiles; but in the context, in which they stand as I have cited them, they seem to have a further meaning, and to embody a great principle, which we all indeed acknowledge, but are deficient in mastering. Under the dispensation of the Spirit all things were to become new and to be reversed. Strength, numbers, wealth, philosophy, eloquence, craft, experience of life, knowledge of human nature, these are the means by which worldly men have ever gained the world. But in that kingdom which Christ has set up, all is contrariwise. 'The weapons of our warfare are not carnal, but mighty through God to the pulling down of strongholds.' What was before in honour, has been dishonoured; what before was in dishonour, has come to honour; what before was successful, fails; what before failed, succeeds. What before was great, has become little; what before was little, has become great. Weakness has conquered strength, for the hidden strength of God 'is made perfect in weakness'. Death has conquered life, for in that death is a more glorious resurrection. Spirit has conquered flesh; for that spirit is an inspiration from above. A new kingdom has been established, not merely different from all kingdoms before it, but contrary to them; a paradox in the eyes of man—the visible rule of the invisible Saviour.

This great change in the history of the world is foretold or described in very many passages of Scripture. Take, for instance, St. Mary's Hymn, which we read every evening; she was no woman of high estate, the nursling of palaces and the pride of a people, yet she was chosen to an illustrious place in the Kingdom of heaven. What God began in her was a sort of type of His dealings with His Church. So she spoke of His 'scattering the proud', 'putting down the mighty', 'exalting the humble and meek', 'filling the hungry with good things', and 'sending the rich empty away'. This was a shadow or outline of that Kingdom of the Spirit, which was then coming on the earth.

Again; when our Lord, in the beginning of His ministry, would declare the great principles and laws of His Kingdom, after what manner did He express Himself? Turn to the Sermon on the Mount. 'He opened His mouth and said, Blessed are the poor in spirit, blessed are they that mourn, blessed are the meek, blessed are they which are persecuted for righteousness' sake'.[1] Poverty was to bring into the Church the riches of the Gentiles; meekness was to conquer the earth; suffering was 'to bind their kings in chains, and their nobles with links of iron'.

On another occasion He added the counterpart:

Woe unto you that are rich! for ye have received your consolation; woe unto you that are full! for ye shall hunger; woe unto you that laugh now! for ye shall mourn and weep; woe unto

[1] Matt. v. 2–10.

you when all men shall speak well of you! for so did their fathers to the false prophets.[1]

St. Paul addresses the Corinthians in the same tone:

Ye see your calling, brethren, how that not many wise men after the flesh, not many mighty, not many noble, are called: but God hath chosen the foolish things of the world to confound the wise; and God hath chosen the weak things of the world to confound the things which are mighty; and base things of the world, and things which are despised, hath God chosen, yea, and things which are not, to bring to nought things that are: that no flesh should glory in His presence.[2]

Once more; consider the Book of Psalms, which, if any part of the Old Testament, belongs immediately to Gospel times, and is the voice of the Christian Church; what is the one idea in that sacred book of devotion from beginning to end? This: that the weak, the oppressed, the defenceless shall be raised to rule the world in spite of its array of might, its threats, and its terrors; that 'the first shall be last, and the last first'.

Such is the kingdom of the sons of God; and while it endures, there is ever a supernatural work going on by which all that man thinks great is overcome, and what he despises prevails.

Yes, so it is; since Christ sent down gifts from on high, the Saints are ever taking possession of the kingdom, and with the weapons of Saints. The invisible powers of the heavens, truth, meekness, and righteousness, are ever coming in upon the earth, ever pouring in, gathering, thronging, warring, triumphing, under the guidance of Him who 'is alive and was dead, and is alive for evermore'. The beloved

[1] Luke vi. 24–26.
[2] 1 Cor. i. 26–29.

disciple saw Him mounted on a white horse, and going forth 'conquering and to conquer'. 'And the armies which were in heaven followed Him upon white horses, clothed in fine linen, white and clean. And out of His mouth goeth a sharp sword, that with it He should smite the nations, and He shall rule them with a rod of iron.'[1]

Now let us apply this great truth to ourselves; for be it ever recollected, *we* are the sons of God, *we* are the soldiers of Christ. The kingdom is within us, and among us, and around us. We are apt to speak of it as a matter of history; we speak of it as at a distance; but really we are a part of it, or ought to be; and, as we wish to be a living portion of it, which is our only hope of salvation, we must learn what its characters are in order to imitate them. It is the characteristic of Christ's Church, that the first should be last, and the last first; are we realizing in ourselves and taking part in this wonderful appointment of God?

Let me explain what I mean: We have most of us by nature longings more or less, and aspirations, after something greater than this world can give. Youth, especially, has a natural love of what is noble and heroic. We like to hear marvellous tales, which throw us out of things as they are, and introduce us to things that are not. We so love the idea of the invisible that we even build fabrics in the air for ourselves, if heavenly truth be not vouchsafed us. We love to fancy ourselves involved in circumstances of danger or trial, and acquitting ourselves well under them. Or we imagine some perfection, such as earth has not, which we follow, and render it our homage and our heart. Such is the state more or less of young persons before the world alters them, before the world comes upon them, as it often does very soon, with its polluting, withering, debasing, deaden-

[1] Rev. xix. 14, 15.

ing influence, before it breathes on them, and blights and parches, and strips off their green foliage, and leaves them, as dry and wintry trees without sap or sweetness. But in early youth we stand with our leaves and blossoms on which promise fruit; we stand by the side of the still waters, with our hearts beating high, with longings after our unknown good, and with a sort of contempt for the fashions of the world; with a contempt for the world, even though we engage in it. Even though we allow ourselves in our degree to listen to it, and to take part in its mere gaieties and amusements, yet we feel the while that our happiness is not there; and we have not yet come to think, though we are in the way to think, that all that is beyond this world is after all an idle dream. We are on our way to think it, for no one stands where he was; his desires after what he has not, his earnest thoughts after things unseen, if not fixed on their true objects, catch at something which he does see, something earthly and perishable, and seduce him from God. But I am speaking of men *before* that time, before they have given their hearts to the world, which promises them true good, then cheats them, and then makes them believe that there is no truth anywhere, and that they were fools for thinking it. But before that time they have desires after things above this world, which they embody in some form of this world, because they have no other way at all of realizing them. If they are in humble life, they dream of becoming their own masters, rising in the world, and securing an independence; if in a higher rank, they have ambitious thoughts of gaining a name and exercising power. While their hearts are thus unsettled, Christ comes to them, if they will receive Him, and promises to satisfy their great need, this hunger and thirst which wearies them. He does not wait till they have learned to ridicule high feelings as mere

R.—F

romantic dreams: He comes to the young; He has them baptized betimes, and then promises them, and in a higher way, those unknown blessings which they yearn after. He seems to say, in the words of the Apostle, 'What ye ignorantly worship, that declare I unto you.' You are seeking what you see not, I give it you; you desire to be great, I will make you so; but observe how—just in the reverse way to what you expect; the way to real glory is to become unknown and despised.

He says, for instance, to the aspiring, as to His two Apostles, 'Whosoever will be great among you, let him be your minister; and whosoever will be chief among you, let him be your servant; even as the Son of man came not to be ministered unto, but to minister.'[1] Here is our rule. The way to mount up is to go down. Every step we take downward makes us higher in the kingdom of heaven. Do you desire to be great? Make yourselves little. There is a mysterious connexion between real advancement and self-abasement. If you minister to the humble and despised, if you feed the hungry, tend the sick, succour the distressed; if you bear with the froward, submit to insult, endure ingratitude, render good for evil, you are, as by a divine charm, getting power over the world and rising among the creatures. God has established this law. Thus He does His wonderful works. His instruments are poor and despised; the world hardly knows their names, or not at all. They are busied about what the world thinks petty actions, and no one minds them. They are apparently set on no great works; nothing is seen to come of what they do: they seem to fail. Nay, even as regards religious objects which they themselves profess to desire, there is no natural and visible connexion between their doings and sufferings and these de-

[1] Matt. xx. 26–28.

sirable ends; but there is an unseen connexion in the kingdom of God. They rise by falling. Plainly so, for no condescension *can* be so great as that of our Lord *Himself*. Now the more they abase themselves the more *like* they are to Him; and the more like they are to Him, the greater must be their power with Him.

When we once recognize this law of God's providence we shall understand better, and be more desirous to imitate, our Lord's precepts, such as the following:

> Ye call Me Master and Lord: and ye say well; for so I am. If I then, your Lord and Master, have washed your feet; ye also ought to wash one another's feet. For I have given you an example, that ye should do as I have done to you. Verily, verily, I say unto you, The servant is not greater than his lord; neither he that is sent greater than he that sent him.

And then our Lord adds, 'If ye know these things, happy are ye if ye do them.'[1] As if He should say to us of this day, You know well that the Gospel was at the first preached and propagated by the poor and lowly against the world's power; you know that fishermen and publicans overcame the world. You know it; you are fond of bringing it forward as an evidence of the truth of the Gospel, and of enlarging on it as something striking, and a topic for many words; happy are ye if ye yourselves fulfil it; happy are ye if *ye* carry on the work of those fishermen; if ye in your generation follow them as they followed Me, and triumph over the world and ascend above it by a like self-abasement.

Again,

> When thou art bidden of any man to a wedding, sit not down in the highest room; . . . but when thou art bidden, go and sit down in the lowest room, that when he that bade thee cometh,

[1] John xiii. 13–17.

he may say unto thee, Friend, go up higher: then shalt thou
have worship in the presence of them that sit at meat with
thee; for whosoever exalteth himself shall be abased, and he
that humbleth himself shall be exalted.[1]

Here is a rule which extends to whatever we do. It is plain
that the spirit of this command leads us, as a condition of
being exalted hereafter, to cultivate here all kinds of little
humiliations; instead of loving display, putting ourselves
forward, seeking to be noticed, being loud or eager in
speech, and bent on having our own way, to be content,
nay, to rejoice in being made little of, to perform what to
the flesh are servile offices, to think it enough to be barely
suffered among men, to be patient under calumny; not to
argue, not to judge, not to pronounce censures, unless a
plain duty comes in; and all this because our Lord has said
that such conduct is the very way to be exalted in His
presence.

Again, 'I say unto you, That ye resist not evil; but whosoever shall smite thee on thy right cheek, turn to him the
other also.'[2] What a precept is this? Why is this voluntary
degradation? What good can come to it? Is it not an ex-
travagance? Not to *resist* evil is going far; but to court it, to
turn the left cheek to the aggressor and to offer to be in-
insulted! What a wonderful command! What? Must we
take pleasure in indignities? Surely we must; however
difficult it be to understand it, however arduous and trying
to practise it. Hear St. Paul's words, which are a comment
on Christ's: 'Therefore I *take pleasure* in infirmities, in reproaches, in necessities, in persecutions, in distresses for
Christ's sake'; he adds the reason; *'for when I am weak, then
am I strong.'*[3] As health and exercise and regular diet are

[1] Luke xiv. 8, 10, 11.
[2] Matt. v. 39.
[3] 2 Cor. xii. 10.

necessary to strength of the body, so an enfeebling and afflicting of the natural man, a chastising and afflicting of soul and body, are necessary to the exaltation of the soul.

Again, St. Paul says, 'Avenge not yourselves, but rather give place unto wrath: for it is written, Vengeance is Mine; I will repay, saith the Lord. Therefore if thine enemy hunger, feed him; if he thirst, give him drink: for in so doing thou shalt heap coals of fire on his head.'[1] As if he said, *This* is a *Christian's* revenge; *this* is how a *Christian* heaps punishment and suffering on the head of his enemy; viz. by returning good for evil. Is there pleasure in seeing an injurer and oppressor at your feet? Has a man wronged you, slandered you, tyrannized over you, abused your confidence, been ungrateful to you? Or to take what is more common, has a man been insolent to you, shown contempt of you, thwarted you, outwitted you, been cruel to you, and you feel resentment—and your feeling is this, 'I wish him no ill, but I should like him just to be brought down for this, and to make amends to me'; rather say, hard though it be,

> I will overcome him with love; except severity be a duty, I will say nothing, do nothing; I will keep quiet, I will seek to do him a service; I owe him a service, not a grudge; and I will be kind, and sweet, and gentle, and composed; and while I cannot disguise from him that I know well where he stands, and where I, still this shall be with all peaceableness and purity of affection.

O hard duty, but most blessed! for even to take into account the *pleasure* of revenge, such as it is, is there not greater gratification in thus melting the proud and injurious heart than in triumphing over it outwardly, without subduing it within? Is there not more of true enjoyment, in looking up

[1] Rom. xii. 19, 20.

to God, and calling Him (so to speak), as a witness of what is done, and having His Angels as conscious spectators of your triumph, though not a soul on earth knows anything of it, than to have your mere carnal retaliation of evil for evil known and talked of, in the presence of all, and more than all, who saw the insult or heard of the wrong?

The case is the same as regards poverty, which it is the fashion of the world to regard not only as the greatest of evils, but as the greatest *disgrace*. Men count it a disgrace, because it certainly does often arise from carelessness, sloth, imprudence, and other faults. But, in many cases, it is nothing else but the very state of life in which God has placed a man; but still, even then, it is equally despised by the world. Now if there is one thing clearly set forth in the Bible it is this, that 'Blessed are the poor'. Our Saviour was the great example of poverty; He was a poor man. St. Paul says, 'Ye know the grace of our Lord Jesus Christ, that, though He was rich, yet for your sakes He became poor, that ye through His poverty might be rich.'[1] Or consider St. Paul's very solemn language about the danger of wealth: 'The love of money is the root of all evil, which while some coveted after, they have erred from the faith, and pierced themselves through with many sorrows.'[2] Can we doubt that poverty is under the Gospel *better* than riches? I say *under* the Gospel, and *in* the regenerate, and *in* the true servants of God. Of course, out of the Gospel, among the unregenerate, among the lovers of this world, it matters not whether one is rich or poor; a man is anyhow unjustified, and there is no better or worse in his outward circumstances. But, I say, *in Christ* the poor is in a more blessed lot than the wealthy. Ever since the Eternal Son of God was born in a

[1] 2 Cor. viii. 9.
[2] 1 Tim. vi. 10.

stable, and had not a place to lay His head, and died an outcast and as a malefactor, heaven has been won by poverty, by disgrace, and by suffering. Not by these things in themselves, but by faith working in and through them.

These are a few out of many things which might be said on this most deep and serious subject. It is strange to say, but it is a truth which our own observation and experience will confirm, that when a man discerns in himself most sin and humbles himself most, when his comeliness seems to him to vanish away and all his graces to wither, when he feels disgust at himself, and revolts at the thought of himself—seems to himself all dust and ashes, all foulness and odiousness, then it is that he is really rising in the kingdom of God: as it is said of Daniel, 'From the first day that thou didst set thine heart to understand and to chasten thyself before thy God, thy words were heard, and I am come for thy words.'[1]

Let us then, my brethren, understand our place, as the redeemed children of God. Some *must* be great in this world, but woe to those who make themselves great; woe to any who take one step out of their way with this object before them. Of course, no one is safe from the intrusion of corrupt motives; but I speak of persons *allowing* themselves in such a motive, and acting mainly from such a motive. Let this be the settled view of all who would promote Christ's cause upon earth. If we are true to ourselves, nothing can really thwart us. Our warfare is not with carnal weapons, but with heavenly. The world does not understand what our real power is, and where it lies. And until we put ourselves into its hands of our own act, it can do nothing against us. Till we leave off patience, meekness, purity, resignation, and peace, it can do nothing against that Truth which is our

[1] Dan. x. 12.

birthright, that Cause which is ours, as it has been the cause of all saints before us. But let all who would labour for God in a dark time beware of anything which ruffles, excites, and in any way withdraws them from the love of God and Christ, and simple obedience to Him.

This be our duty in the dark night, while we wait for the day; while we wait for Him who is our Day, while we wait for His coming, who is gone, who will return, and before whom all the tribes of the earth will mourn, but the sons of God will rejoice. 'It doth not yet appear what we shall be: but we know that, when He shall appear, we shall be like Him; for we shall see Him as He is. And every man that hath this hope in Him purifieth himself, even as He is pure.'[1] It is our blessedness to be made like the all-holy, all-gracious, long-suffering, and merciful God; who made and who redeemed us; in whose presence is perfect rest, and perfect peace; whom the Seraphim are harmoniously praising, and the Cherubim tranquilly contemplating, and Angels silently serving, and the Church thankfully worshipping. All is order, repose, love, and holiness in heaven. There is no anxiety, no ambition, no resentment, no discontent, no bitterness, no remorse, no tumult. 'Thou wilt keep him in perfect peace, whose mind is stayed on Thee: because He trusteth in Thee. Trust ye in the Lord for ever: for in the Lord Jehovah is everlasting strength.'[2]*

[1] I John iii. 2, 3.
[2] Isa. xxvi. 3, 4.

*'The Weapons of Saints', *PPS*, VI, Sermon 22.

# 6. CHRISTIAN SINCERITY

## UNREAL WORDS
### (ADVENT)

*ISAIAH XXXIII. 17*
*'Thine eyes shall see the King in His beauty; they shall behold the land*
*that is very far off.'*

THE Prophet tells us that under the Gospel covenant
God's servants will have the privilege of seeing those
heavenly sights which were but shadowed out in the Law.
Before Christ came was the time of shadows; but when He
came, He brought truth as well as grace; and as He who is
the Truth has come to us, so does He in return require that
we should be true and sincere in our dealings with Him. To
be true and sincere is really to see with our minds those
great wonders which He has wrought in order that we might
see them. When God opened the eyes of the ass on which
Balaam rode, she saw the Angel and acted upon the sight.
When He opened the eyes of the young man, Elisha's servant, he too saw the chariots and horses of fire, and took
comfort. And in like manner, Christians are now under the
protection of a Divine Presence, and that more wonderful
than any which was vouchsafed of old time. God revealed
Himself visibly to Jacob, to Job, to Moses, to Joshua, and
to Isaiah; to us He reveals Himself not visibly, but more
wonderfully and truly; not without the co-operation of our
own will, but upon our faith, and for that very reason more
truly; for faith is the special means of gaining spiritual

blessings. Hence St. Paul prays for the Ephesians 'that Christ
may dwell in their hearts by faith', and that 'the eyes of
their understanding may be enlightened'. And St. John
declares that 'the Son of God hath given us an understanding that we may know Him that is true: and we are
in Him that is true, even in His Son Jesus Christ.'[1]

We are no longer then in the region of shadows: we have
the true Saviour set before us, the true reward, and the true
means of spiritual renewal. We know the true state of the
soul by nature and by grace, the evil of sin, the consequences
of sinning, the way of pleasing God, and the motives to act
upon. God has revealed Himself clearly to us; He has 'destroyed the face of the covering cast over all people, and the
veil that is spread over all nations'. 'The darkness is past,
and the True Light now shineth.'[2] And therefore, I say,
He calls upon us in turn to 'walk in the light as He is in the
light'. The Pharisees might have this excuse in their
hypocrisy, that the plain truth had not been revealed to
them; we have not even this poor reason for insincerity.
We have no opportunity of mistaking one thing for another:
the promise is expressly made to us that 'our teachers shall
not be removed into a corner any more, but our eyes shall
see our teachers'; that 'the eyes of them that see shall not
be dim'; that everything shall be called by its right name;
that 'the vile person shall be no more called liberal, nor the
churl said to be bountiful';[3] in a word, as the text speaks,
that 'our eyes shall see the King in His beauty; we shall
behold the land that is very far off'. Our professions, our
creeds, our prayers, our dealings, our conversation, our
arguments, our teaching must henceforth be sincere, or, to

[1] Ephes. iii. 17; i. 18; 1 John v. 20.
[2] Isa. xxv. 7; 1 John ii. 8.
[3] Isa. xxx. 20; xxxii. 3, 5.

use an expressive word, must be *real*. What St. Paul says of himself and his fellow labourers, that they were true because Christ is true, applies to all Christians:

> Our rejoicing is this, the testimony of our conscience, that in simplicity and godly sincerity, not with fleshly wisdom, but by the grace of God, we have had our conversation in the world, and more abundantly to youward. . . . The things that I purpose, do I purpose according to the flesh, that with me there should be yea yea, and nay nay? But as God is true, our word toward you was not yea and nay. For the Son of God, Jesus Christ, . . . was not yea and nay, but in Him was yea. For all the promises of God in Him are yea, and in Him Amen, unto the glory of God by us.[1]

And yet, it need scarcely be said, nothing is so rare as honesty and singleness of mind; so much so, that a person who is really honest, is already perfect. Insincerity was an evil which sprang up within the Church from the first; Ananias and Simon were not open opposers of the Apostles, but false brethren. And, as foreseeing what was to be, our Saviour is remarkable in His ministry for nothing more than the earnestness of the dissuasives which He addressed to those who came to Him, against taking up religion lightly, or making promises which they were likely to break.

Thus He, 'the True Light, which lighteth every man that cometh into the world', 'the Amen, the faithful and true Witness, the Beginning of the creation of God',[2] said to the young Ruler, who lightly called Him 'Good Master', 'Why callest thou Me good?' as bidding him weigh his words; and then abruptly told him, 'One thing thou lackest.' When a certain man professed that he would follow Him whithersoever He went, He did not respond to

---

[1] 2 Cor. i. 12–20.
[2] John i. 9; Rev. iii. 14.

him, but said, 'The foxes have holes, and the birds of the air have nests, but the Son of Man hath not where to lay His head.' When St. Peter said with all his heart in the name of himself and brethren, 'To whom shall we go? Thou hast the words of eternal life', He answered pointedly, 'Have not I chosen you twelve, and one of you is a devil?' as if He said, 'Answer for thyself.' When the two Apostles professed their desire to cast their lot with Him, He asked whether they could 'drink of His cup, and be baptized with His baptism'. And when 'there went great multitudes with Him', He turned and said, that unless a man hated relations, friends, and self, he could not be His disciple. And then he proceeded to warn all men to 'count the cost' ere they followed him. Such is the merciful severity with which He repels us that He may gain us more truly. And what He thinks of those who, after coming to Him, relapse into a hollow and hypocritical profession, we learn from His language towards the Laodiceans: 'I know thy works, that thou art neither cold nor hot: I would thou wert cold or hot. So then, because thou art lukewarm, and neither cold not hot, I will cast thee out of My mouth.'[1]

We have a striking instance of the same conduct on the part of that ancient Saint who prefigured our Lord in name and office, Joshua, the captain of the chosen people in entering Canaan. When they had at length taken possession of that land which Moses and their fathers had seen 'very far off', they said to him, 'God forbid that we should forsake the Lord, and serve other gods. We will . . . serve the Lord, for He is our God.' He made answer, 'Ye cannot serve the Lord; for He is a holy God; He is a jealous God; He will not forgive your transgressions nor your sins.'[2] Not

---

[1] Mark x. 17–21; Matt. viii. 20; John vi. 68–70; Matt. xx. 22; Luke xiv. 25–28; Rev. iii. 15, 16.
[2] Josh. xxiv. 16–19.

as if he would hinder them from obeying, but to sober them in professing. How does his answer remind us of St. Paul's still more awful words, about the impossibility of renewal after utterly falling away!

And what is said of profession of *discipleship* applies undoubtedly in its degree to *all* profession. To make professions is to play with edged tools, unless we attend to what we are saying. Words have a meaning, whether we mean that meaning or not; and they are imputed to us in their real meaning, when our not meaning it is our own fault. He who takes God's Name in vain, is not counted guiltless because he means nothing by it—he cannot frame a language for himself; and they who make professions, of whatever kind, are heard in the sense of those professions, and are not excused because they themselves attach no sense to them. 'By thy words thou shalt be justified, and by thy words thou shalt be condemned.'[1]

Now this consideration needs especially to be pressed upon Christians at this day; for this is especially a day of professions. You will answer in my own words, that all ages have been ages of profession. So they have been, in one way or other, but this day in its own especial sense—because this is especially a day of individual profession. This is a day in which there is (rightly or wrongly) so much of private judgment, so much of separation and difference, so much of preaching and teaching, so much of authorship, that it involves individual profession, responsibility, and recompense in a way peculiarly its own. It will not then be out of place if, in connexion with the text, we consider some of the many ways in which persons, whether in this age or in another, make unreal professions, or seeing see not, and hearing hear not, and speak without mastering, or trying

[1] Matt. xii. 37.

to master, their words. This I will attempt to do at some length, and in matters of detail, which are not the less important because they are minute.

Of course, it is very common in all matters, not only in religion, to speak in an unreal way; viz. when we speak on a subject with which our minds are not familiar. If you were to hear a person who knew nothing about military matters giving directions how soldiers on service should conduct themselves, or how their food and lodging, or their marching, was to be duly arranged, you would be sure that his mistakes would be such as to excite the ridicule and contempt of men experienced in warfare. If a foreigner were to come to one of our cities, and without hesitation offer plans for the supply of our markets, or the management of our police, it is so certain that he would expose himself, that the very attempt would argue a great want of good sense and modesty. We should feel that he did not understand us, and that when he spoke about us he would be using words without meaning. If a dim-sighted man were to attempt to decide questions of a proportion and colour, or a man without ear to judge of musical compositions, we should feel that he spoke on and from general principles, on fancy, or by deduction and argument, not from a real apprehension of the matters which he discussed. His remarks would be theoretical and unreal.

This unsubstantial way of speaking is instanced in the case of persons who fall into any new company, among strange faces and amid novel occurrences. They sometimes form amiable judgments of men and things, sometimes the reverse—but whatever their judgments be, they are to those who know the men and the things strangely unreal and distorted. They feel reverence where they should not; they discern slights where none were intended; they discover meaning in events which have none; they fancy motives; they misinterpret manner; they mistake character; and they form generalizations and combinations which exist only in their own minds.

Again, persons who have not attended to the subject of morals, or to politics, or to matters ecclesiastical, or to theology, do not know the relative value of questions which they meet with in these departments of knowledge. They do not understand the difference between one point and another. The one and the other are the same to them. They look at them as infants gaze at the objects which meet their eyes, in a vague unapprehensive way, as if not knowing whether a thing is a hundred miles off or close at hand, whether great or small, hard or soft. They have no means of judging, no standard to measure by—and they give judgment at random, saying yea or nay on very deep questions, according as their fancy is struck at the moment, or as some clever or specious argument happens to come across them. Consequently they are inconsistent; say one thing one day, another the next—and if they must act, act in the dark; or if they can help acting, do not act; or if they act freely, act from some other reason not avowed. All this is to be unreal.

Again, there cannot be a more apposite specimen of unreality than the way in which judgments are commonly formed upon important questions by the mass of the community. Opinions are continually given in the world on matters, about which those who offer them are as little qualified to judge as blind men about colours, and that because they have never exercised their minds upon the points in question. This is a day in which all men are obliged to have an opinion on all questions, political, social, and religious, because they have in some way or other an influence upon the decision; yet the multitude are for the most part absolutely without capacity to take their part in it. In saying this, I am far from meaning that this need be so—I am far from denying that there is such a thing as plain good sense, or (what is better) religious sense, which will see its way through very intricate matters, or that this is in fact sometimes exerted in the community at large on certain great questions; but at the same time this practical sense is so far from existing as regards the vast mass of questions which in this day come before the public that (as all persons who attempt to gain the influence of the people on their side know well) their opinions must be purchased by interesting their prejudices or fears in their favour—not by presenting a question in its real and true substance, but by adroitly colouring it, or selecting out of it some particular point which may be exaggerated, and dressed up, and be made the means of working on popular feelings. And thus government and the art of government becomes, as much as popular religion, hollow and unsound.

And hence it is that the popular voice is so changeable. One man or measure is the idol of the people today, another tomorrow. They have never got beyond accepting shadows for things.

What is instanced in the mass is instanced also in various ways in individuals, and in points of detail. For instance, some men are set perhaps on being eloquent speakers. They use great words and imitate the sentences of others; and they fancy that those whom they imitate had as little meaning as themselves or they perhaps contrive to think that they themselves have a meaning adequate to their words.

Another sort of unreality, or voluntary profession of what is above us, is instanced in the conduct of those who suddenly come into power or place. They affect a manner such as they think the office requires, but which is beyond them, and therefore unbecoming. They wish to act with dignity, and they cease to be themselves.

And so again, to take a different case, many men, when they come near persons in distress and wish to show sympathy, often condole in a very unreal way. I am not altogether laying this to their fault; for it is very difficult to know what to do, when on the one hand we cannot realize to ourselves the sorrow, yet withal wish to be kind to those who feel it. A tone of grief seems necessary, yet (if so be) cannot under our circumstances be genuine. Yet even here surely there is a true way, if we could find it, by which pretence may be avoided, and yet respect and consideration shown.

And in like manner as regards religious emotions. Persons are aware from the mere force of the doctrines of which the Gospel consists, that they ought to be variously affected, and deeply and intensely too, in consequence of them. The doctrines of original and actual sin, of Christ's Divinity and Atonement, and of Holy Baptism, are so vast, that no one can realize them without very complicated and profound feelings. Natural reason tells a man this, and that if he simply and genuinely believes the doctrines, he must have these feelings; and he professes to believe the doctrines absolutely, and therefore he professes the correspondent feelings. But in truth he perhaps does *not* really believe them absolutely, because such absolute belief is the work of long time, and therefore his profession of feeling outruns the real inward existence of feeling, or he becomes unreal. Let us never lose sight of two truths—that we ought to have our hearts penetrated with the love of Christ and full of self-renunciation; but that if they be not, professing that they are does not make them so.

Again, to take a more serious instance of the same fault,

some persons pray, not as sinners addressing their God, not as the Publican smiting on his breast, and saying, 'God be merciful to me a sinner', but in such a way as they conceive to be becoming *under* circumstances of guilt, in a way becoming such a strait. They are self-conscious, and reflect on what they are about, and instead of actually approaching (as it were) the mercy-seat, they are filled with the thought that God is great, and man His creature, God on high and man on earth, and that they are engaged in a high and solemn service, and that they ought to rise up to its sublime and momentous character.

Another still more common form of the same fault, yet without any definite pretence or effort, is the mode in which people speak of the shortness and vanity of life, the certainty of death, and the joys of heaven. They have commonplaces in their mouths, which they bring forth upon occasions for the good of others, or to console them, or as a proper and becoming mark of attention towards them. Thus they speak to clergymen in a professedly serious way, making remarks true and sound, and in themselves deep, yet unmeaning in their mouths; or they give advice to children or young men; or perhaps in low spirits or sickness they are led to speak in a religious strain as if it was spontaneous. Or when they fall into sin, they speak of man being frail, of the deceitfulness of the human heart, of God's mercy, and so on —all these great words, heaven, hell, judgment, mercy, repentance, works, the world that now is, the world to come, being little more than 'lifeless sounds, whether of pipe or harp', in their mouths and ears, as the 'very lovely song of one that hath a pleasant voice and can play well on an instrument'—as the proprieties of conversation, or the civilities of good breeding.

I am speaking of the conduct of the world at large,

called Christian; but what has been said applies, and necessarily, to the case of a number of well-disposed or even religious men. I mean, that before men come to know the realities of human life, it is not wonderful that their view of religion should be unreal. Young people who have never known sorrow or anxiety, or the sacrifices which conscientiousness involves, want commonly that depth and seriousness of character, which sorrow only and anxiety and self-sacrifice can give. I do not notice this as a fault, but as a plain fact, which may often be seen, and which it is well to bear in mind. This is the legitimate use of this world, to make us seek for another. It does its part when it repels us and disgusts us and drives us elsewhere. Experience of it gives experience of that which is its antidote, in the case of religious minds; and we become real in our view of what is spiritual by the contact of things temporal and earthly. And much more are men unreal when they have some secret motive urging them a different way from religion, and when their professions therefore are forced into an unnatural course in order to subserve their secret motive. When men do not like the conclusions to which their principles lead, or the precepts which Scripture contains, they are not wanting in ingenuity to blunt their force. They can frame some theory, or dress up certain objections, to defend themselves withal; a theory, that is, or objections, which it is difficult to refute perhaps, but which any rightly-ordered mind, nay, any common bystander, perceives to be unnatural and insincere.

What has been here noticed of individuals takes place even in the case of whole Churches, at times when love has waxed cold and faith failed. The whole system of the Church, its discipline and ritual, are all in their origin the spontaneous and exuberant fruit of the real principle of spiritual religion in the hearts of its members. The invisible Church has developed itself into the Church visible, and its outward rites and forms are nourished and animated by the living power which dwells within it. Thus every part of it is real, down to the minutest details. But when the seductions of the world and the lusts of the flesh have eaten out this divine inward life, what is the outward Church but a hollowness and a mockery, like the whited sepulchres of which our Lord speaks, a memorial of what was and is not? And though we trust that the Church is nowhere thus utterly deserted by the Spirit of truth, at least according to God's ordinary providence, yet may we not say that in proportion as it approaches to this state of deadness, the grace of its ordinances, though not forfeited, at least flows in but a scanty or uncertain stream?

And lastly, if this unreality may steal over the Church itself, which is in its very essence a practical institution, much more is it found in the philosophies and literature of men. Literature is almost in its essence unreal; for it is the exhibition of thought disjoined from practice. Its very home is supposed to be ease and retirement; and when it does more than speak or write, it is accused of transgressing its bounds. This indeed constitutes what is considered its true dignity and honour, viz. its abstraction from the actual affairs of life; its security from the world's currents and vicissitudes; its saying without doing. A man of literature is considered to preserve his dignity by doing nothing; and when he proceeds forward into action, he is thought to lose his position, as if he were degrading his calling by enthusiasm, and becoming a politician or a partisan. Hence mere literary men are able to say strong things against the opinions of their age, whether religious or political, without offence; because no one thinks they mean anything by them. They are not expected to go foward to act upon them, and mere words hurt no one.

Such are some of the more common or more extended specimens of profession without action, or of speaking without really seeing and feeling. In instancing which, let it be observed, I do not mean to say that such profession, as has been described, is always culpable and wrong; indeed I have implied the contrary throughout. It is often a misfortune. It takes a long time really to feel and understand things as they are; we learn to do so only gradually. Profession beyond our feelings is only a fault when we might help it—when either we speak when we need not speak, or do not feel when we might have felt. Hard insensible hearts, ready and thoughtless talkers, these are they whose unreality, as I have termed it, is a sin; it is the sin of every one of us, in proportion as our hearts are cold, or our tongues excessive.

But the mere fact of our saying more than we feel is not necessarily sinful. St. Peter did not rise up to the full meaning of his confession. 'Thou art the Christ', yet he was pronounced blessed. St. James and St. John said, 'We are able', without clear apprehension, yet without offence. We ever promise things greater than we master, and we wait on God to enable us to perform them. Our promising involves a prayer for light and strength. And so again we all say the Creed, but who comprehends it fully? All we can hope is, that we are in the way to understand it; that we partly understand it; that we desire, pray, and strive to understand it more and more. Our Creed becomes a sort of prayer. Persons are culpably unreal in their way of speaking, not when they say more than they feel, but when they say things different from what they feel. A miser praising almsgiving, or a coward giving rules for courage, is unreal; but it is not unreal for the less to discourse about the greater, for the liberal to descant upon munificence, or the generous to praise the noble-minded, or the self-denying to use the language of the austere, or the confessor to exhort to martyrdom.

What I have been saying comes to this—be in earnest, and you will speak of religion where, and when, and how you should; aim at things, and your words will be right without aiming. There are ten thousand ways of looking at this world, but only one right way. The man of pleasure has his way, the man of gain his, and the man of intellect his. Poor men and rich men, governors and governed, prosperous and discontented, learned and unlearned, each has his own way of looking at the things which come before him, and each has a wrong way. There is but one right way; it is the way in which God looks at the world. Aim at looking at it in God's way. Aim at seeing things as God sees them. Aim at forming judgments about persons, events, ranks, fortunes, changes, objects, such as God forms. Aim at looking at this life as God looks at it. Aim at looking at the life to come, and the world unseen, as God does. Aim at 'seeing the King in His beauty'. All things that we see are but shadows to us and delusions, unless we enter into what they really mean.

It is not an easy thing to learn that new language which Christ has brought us. He has interpreted all things for us in a new way; He has brought us a religion which sheds a new light on all that happens. Try to learn this language. Do not get it by rote, or speak it as a thing of course. Try to understand what you say. Time is short, eternity is long; God is great, man is weak; he stands between heaven and hell; Christ is his Saviour; Christ has suffered for him. The

Holy Ghost sanctifies him; repentance purifies him, faith justifies, works save. These are solemn truths, which need not be actually spoken, except in the way of creed or of teaching; but which must be laid up in the heart. That a thing is true is no reason that it should be said, but that it should be done; that it should be acted upon; that it should be made our own inwardly.

Let us avoid talking, of whatever kind; whether mere empty talking, or censorious talking, or idle profession, or descanting upon Gospel doctrines, or the affectation of philosophy, or the pretence of eloquence. Let us guard against frivolity, love of display, love of being talked about, love of singularity, love of seeming original. Let us aim at meaning what we say, and saying what we mean; let us aim at knowing when we understand a truth, and when we do not. When we do not, let us take it on faith, and let us profess to do so. Let us receive the truth in reverence, and pray God to give us a good will, and divine light, and spiritual strength, that it may bear fruit within us.*

*'Unreal Words', *PPS*, V, Sermon 3.

# 7. THE CHRISTIAN DEBT

## REMEMBRANCE OF PAST MERCIES

### (CHRISTMAS)

*GEN. XXXII. 10*
*'I am not worthy of the least of all the mercies, and of all the truth, which Thou hast showed unto Thy servant.'*

THE spirit of humble thankfulness for past mercies which these words imply is a grace to which we are especially called in the Gospel. Jacob, who spoke them, knew not of those great and wonderful acts of love with which God has since visited the race of man. But though he might not know the depths of God's counsels, he knew himself so far as to know that he was worthy of no good thing at all, and he knew also that Almighty God had shown him great mercies and great truth: mercies, in that He had done for him good things, whereas he had deserved evil; and truth, in that He had made him promises, and had been faithful to them. In consequence, he overflowed with gratitude when he looked back upon the past; marvelling at the contrast between what he was in himself and what God had been to him.

Such thankfulness, I say, is eminently a Christian grace, and is enjoined on us in the New Testament. For instance, we are exhorted to be 'thankful', and to let 'the Word of Christ dwell in us richly in all wisdom; teaching and admonishing one another in psalms and hymns and spiritual songs, singing with grace in our hearts to the Lord'.

Elsewhere, we are told to 'speak to ourselves in psalms and hymns and spiritual songs, singing and making melody in our heart to the Lord: giving thanks always for all things unto God and the Father, in the Name of our Lord Jesus Christ'.

Again: 'Be careful for nothing: but in every thing by prayer and supplication, with thanksgiving, let your requests be made known unto God.'

Again: 'In every thing give thanks: for this is the will of God in Christ Jesus concerning you.'[1]

The Apostle, who writes all this, was himself an especial pattern of a thankful spirit: 'Rejoice in the Lord alway,' he says: 'and again I say, Rejoice.' 'I have learned, in whatsoever state I am, therewith to be content. I have all and abound; I am full.' Again:

> I thank Christ Jesus our Lord, who hath enabled me, for that He counted me faithful, putting me into the ministry; who was before a blasphemer, and a persecutor, and injurious. But I obtained mercy, because I did it ignorantly in unbelief. And the grace of our Lord was exceeding abundant, with faith and love which is in Christ Jesus.[2]

O great Apostle! how could it be otherwise, considering what he had been and what he was—transformed from an enemy to a friend, from a blind Pharisee to an inspired preacher? And yet there is another Saint, besides the patriarch Jacob, who is his fellow in this excellent grace—like them, distinguished by great vicissitudes of life, and by the adoring love and the tenderness of heart with which he

---

[1] Col. iii. 15, 16; Eph. v. 19, 20; Phil. iv. 6; 1 Thess. v. 18.
[2] Phil. iv. 4, 11, 18; 1 Tim. i. 12–14.

looked back upon the past: I mean, 'David, the son of Jesse, the man who was raised up on high, the anointed of the God of Jacob, and the sweet Psalmist of Israel.'[1]

The Book of Psalms is full of instances of David's thankful spirit, which I need not cite here, as we are all so well acquainted with them. I will but refer to his thanksgiving, when he set apart the precious materials for the building of the Temple, as it occurs at the end of the First Book of Chronicles; when he rejoiced so greatly, because he and his people had the heart to offer freely to God, and thanked God for his very thankfulness.

> David, the king . . . rejoiced with great joy; wherefore David blessed the Lord before all the congregation; and David said, Blessed be Thou, Lord God of Israel, our Father, for ever and ever. . . . Both riches and honour come of Thee, and Thou reignest over all; and in Thine hand is power and might, and in Thine hand it is to make great, and to give strength unto all. Now, therefore, our God, we thank Thee, and praise Thy glorious Name. But who am I, and what is my people, that we should be able to offer so willingly after this sort? for all things come of Thee, and of Thine own have we given Thee.[2]

Such was the thankful spirit of David, looking back upon the past, wondering and rejoicing at the way in which his Almighty Protector had led him on, and at the works He had enabled him to do; and praising and glorifying Him for His mercy and truth. David, then, Jacob, and St. Paul, may be considered the three great patterns of thankfulness, which are set before us in Scripture; saints, all of whom were peculiarly the creation of God's grace, and whose very life and breath it was humbly and adoringly to meditate upon the contrast between what, in different ways, they

[1] 2 Sam. xxiii. 1.
[2] 1 Chron. xxix. 9–14.

had been, and what they were. A perishing wanderer had unexpectedly become a patriarch; a shepherd, a king; and a persecutor, an apostle: each had been chosen, at God's inscrutable pleasure, to fulfil a great purpose, and each, while he did his utmost to fulfil it, kept praising God that he was made His instrument. Of the first, it was said, 'Jacob have I loved, but Esau have I hated'; of the second, that 'He refused the tabernacle of Joseph, and chose not the tribe of Ephraim, but chose the tribe of Judah, even the hill of Sion, which He loved: He chose David also His servant, and took him away from the sheepfolds.' And St. Paul says of himself, 'Last of all, He was seen of me also, as of one born out of due time.'[1]

These thoughts naturally come over the mind at this season, when we are engaged in celebrating God's grace in making us His children, by the incarnation of His Only-begotten Son, the greatest and most wonderful of all His mercies. And to the Patriarch Jacob our minds are now particularly turned, by the First Lessons for this day,[2] taken from the Prophet Isaiah, in which the Church is addressed and comforted under the name of Jacob. Let us then, in this season of thankfulness, and at the beginning of a new year, take a brief view of the character of this Patriarch; and though David and Isaiah be the prophets of grace, and St. Paul its special herald and chief pattern, yet, if we wish to see an actual specimen of a habit of thankfulness occupied in the remembrance of God's mercies, I think we shall not be wrong in betaking ourselves to Jacob.

Jacob's distinguishing grace then, as I think it may be called, was a habit of affectionate musing upon God's providences towards him in times past, and of overflowing

[1] Rom. ix. 13; Ps. lxxviii. 68–71; 1 Cor. xv. 8.
[2] Second Sunday after Christmas.

thankfulness for them. Not that he had not other graces also, but this seems to have been his distinguishing grace. All good men have in their measure all graces; for He, by whom they have any, does not give one apart from the whole: He gives the root, and the root puts forth branches. But since time, and circumstances, and their own use of the gift, and their own disposition and character, have much influence on the mode of its manifestation, so it happens, that each good man has his own distinguishing grace, apart from the rest, his own particular hue and frag-rance and fashion, as a flower may have. As, then, there are numberless flowers on the earth, all of them flowers, and so far like each other; and all springing from the same earth, and nourished by the same air and dew, and none without beauty; and yet some are more beautiful than others; and of those which are beautiful, some excel in colour, and others in sweetness, and others in form; and then, again, those which are sweet have such perfect sweetness, yet so distinct, that we do not know how to compare them together, or to say which is the sweeter: so is it with souls filled and nur-tured by God's secret grace. Abraham, for instance, Jacob's forefather, was the pattern of faith. This is insisted on in Scripture, and it is not here necessary to show that he was so. It will be sufficient to say, that he left his country at God's word; and, at the same word, took up the knife to slay his own son. Abraham seems to have had something very noble and magnanimous about him. He could realize and make present to him things unseen. He followed God in the dark as promptly, as firmly, with as cheerful a heart, and bold a stepping, as if he were in broad daylight. There is something very great in this; and, therefore, St. Paul calls Abraham *our* father, the father of Christians as well as of Jews. For we are especially bound to walk by faith, not by sight; and are

blessed in faith, and justified by faith, as was faithful
Abraham. Now (if I may say it, with due reverence to the
memory of that favoured servant of God, in whose praise I
am now speaking) that faith in which Abraham excelled
was not Jacob's characteristic excellence. Not that he had
not faith, and great faith, else he would not have been so
dear to God. His buying the birthright and gaining the
blessing from Esau were proofs of faith. Esau saw nothing
or little precious in them—he was profane; easily parted
with the one, and had no high ideas of the other. However,
Jacob's faith, earnest and vigorous as it was, was not like
Abraham's. Abraham kept his affections loose from everything earthly, and was ready, at God's word, to slay his only
son. Jacob had many sons, and may we not even say that he
indulged them overmuch?" Even as regards Joseph, whom
he so deservedly loved, beautiful and touching as his love
of him is, yet there is a great contrast between his feelings
towards the 'son of his old age' and those of Abraham
towards Isaac, the unexpected offspring of his hundredth
year—nor only such, but his long-promised only son, with
whom were the promises. Again: Abraham left his country
—so did Jacob; but Abraham, at God's word—Jacob, from
necessity on the threat of Esau. Abraham, from the first, felt
that God was his portion and his inheritance, and, in a
great and generous spirit, he freely gave up all he had, being
sure that he should find what was more excellent in doing
so. But Jacob, in spite of his really living by faith, wished (if
we may so say), as one passage of his history shows, to see
before he fully believed. When he was escaping from Esau
and came to Bethel, and God appeared to him in a dream
and gave him promises, but not yet the performance of
them—what did he do? Did he simply accept them? He
says, '*If* God will be with me, and will keep me in this way

that I go, and will give me bread to eat, and raiment to put on, so that I come again to my father's house in peace, *then* shall the Lord be my God.'[1] He makes his obedience, in some sense, depend on a condition; and although we must not, and need not, take the words as if he meant that he would not serve God *till* and *unless* He did for him what He had promised, yet they seem to show a fear and anxiety, gentle indeed, and subdued, and very human (and therefore the more interesting and winning in the eyes of us common men, who read his words), yet an anxiety which Abraham had not. We feel Jacob to be more like ourselves than Abraham was.

What, then, was Jacob's distinguishing grace, as faith was Abraham's? I have already said it: I suppose, thankfulness. Abraham appears ever to have been looking forward in *hope*—Jacob looking back in *memory*: the one rejoicing in the future, the other in the past; the one setting his affections on the future, the other on the past; the one making his way towards the promises, the other musing over their fulfilment. Not that Abraham did not look back also, and Jacob, as he says on his death-bed, did not 'wait for the salvation' of God; but this was the difference between them, Abraham was a hero, Jacob 'a plain man, dwelling in tents'.

Jacob seems to have had a gentle, tender, affectionate, timid mind—easily frightened, easily agitated, loving God so much that he feared to lose Him, and, like St. Thomas perhaps, anxious for sight and possession from earnest and longing desire of them. Were it not for faith, love would become impatient, and thus Jacob desired to possess, not from cold incredulity or hardness of heart, but from such a loving impatience. Such men are easily downcast, and must

[1] Gen. xxviii. 20, 21.

be treated kindly; they soon despond, they shrink from the world, for they feel its rudeness, which bolder natures do not. Neither Abraham nor Jacob loved the world. But Abraham did not fear, did not feel it. Jacob felt and winced, as being wounded by it. You recollect his touching complaints, 'All these things are against me!'—'Then shall ye bring down my grey hairs with sorrow to the grave.'— 'If I am bereaved of my children, I am bereaved.' Again, elsewhere we are told, 'All his sons and all his daughters rose up to comfort him, but he refused to be comforted.' At another time, 'Jacob's heart fainted, for he believed them not.' Again, 'The spirit of Jacob their father revived.'[1] You see what a child-like, sensitive, sweet mind he had. Accordingly, as I have said, his happiness lay, not in looking forward to the hope, but backwards upon the experience, of God's mercies towards him. He delighted lovingly to trace, and gratefully to acknowledge, what had been given, leaving the future to itself.

For instance, when coming to meet Esau, he brings before God in prayer, in words of which the text is part, what He had already done for him, recounting His past favours with great and humble joy in the midst of his present anxiety.

O God of my father Abraham [he says], and God of my father Isaac, the Lord which saidst unto me, Return unto thy country, and to thy kindred, and I will deal well with thee: I am not worthy of the least of all the mercies, and of all the truth, *which Thou hast showed unto Thy servant; for with my staff I passed over this Jordan, and now I am become two bands.*

Again, after he had returned to his own land, he proceeded to fulfil the promise he had made to consecrate Bethel as a

[1] Gen. xlii. 36, 38; xliii. 14; xxxvii. 35; xlv. 26, 27.

house of God, 'Let us arise, and go up to Bethel; and I will make there an altar unto God, *who answered me in the day of my distress, and was with me in the way which I went.*' Again, to Pharaoh, still dwelling on the past: 'The days of the years of my pilgrimage are an hundred and thirty years; few and evil have the days of the years of my life been,' he means, in themselves, and as separate from God's favour, 'and have not attained unto the days of the years of the life of my fathers, in the days of their pilgrimage'. Again, when he was approaching his end, he says to Joseph, 'God Almighty *appeared unto me* at Luz', that is, Bethel, 'in the land of Canaan, and blessed me'. Again, still looking back, 'As for me, when I came from Padan, Rachel died by me in the land of Canaan, in the way, when yet there was but a little way to come to Ephrath; and I buried her there in the way of Ephrath.' Again, his blessing upon Ephraim and Manasseh: 'God, before whom my fathers Abraham and Isaac did walk, *the God which fed me all my life long unto this day*, the Angel which redeemed me from all evil, bless the lads.' Again he looks back on the land of promise, though in the plentifulness of Egypt: 'Behold, I die, but God shall be with you, and bring you again unto the land of your fathers.' And when he gives command about his burial, he says: 'I am to be gathered unto my people; bury me with my fathers in the cave that is in the field of Ephron the Hittite.' He gives orders to be buried with his fathers; this was natural, but observe, he goes on to *enlarge* on the subject, after his special manner: 'There they buried Abraham and Sarah his wife; there they buried Isaac and Rebekah his wife; and *there I buried Leah.*' And further on, when he speaks of waiting for God's salvation, which is an act of hope, he so words it as at the same time to dwell upon the past: 'I *have* waited,' he says, that is, all my life long, 'I have waited for Thy salvation, O Lord.'[1] Such was Jacob, living in memory rather than in hope, counting times, recording seasons, keeping days; having his history by heart, and his past life in his hand; and as if to carry on his mind into that of his descendants, it was enjoined upon them, that once a year every Israelite should appear before God with a basket of fruit of the earth, and call to mind what God had done for him and his father Jacob, and express his thankfulness for it.

A Syrian ready to perish was my father [he had to say, meaning Jacob]; and he went down into Egypt, and sojourned there, and became a nation, great, mighty, and populous. . . . And the Lord brought us forth out of Egypt with an outstretched arm, and with great terribleness, and with signs, and with wonders; and hath brought us into this land . . . that floweth with milk and honey. And now, behold, I have brought the first-fruits of the land, which Thou, O Lord, hast given me.[2]

Well were it for us, if we had the character of mind instanced in Jacob, and enjoined on his descendants; the temper of dependence upon God's providence, and thankfulness under it, and careful memory of all He has done for us. It would be well if we were in the habit of looking at all we have as God's gift, undeservedly given, and day by day continued to us solely by His mercy. He gave; He may take away. He gave us all we have, life, health, strength, reason, enjoyment, the light of conscience; whatever we have good and holy within us; whatever faith we have; whatever of a renewed will; whatever love towards Him; whatever power over ourselves; whatever prospect of heaven. He gave us relatives, friends, education, training, knowledge, the Bible,

[1] Gen. xxxii. 9, 10; xxxv. 3; xlvii. 9; xlviii. 3, 7, 15, 16, 21; xlix. 29–31, 18.
[2] Deut. xxvi. 5–10.

R.—H

the Church. All comes from Him. He gave; He may take away. Did He take away, we should be called on to follow Job's pattern, and be resigned: 'The Lord gave, and the Lord hath taken away. Blessed be the Name of the Lord.'[1] While He continues His blessings, we should follow David and Jacob, by living in constant praise and thanksgiving, and in offering up to Him of His own.

We are not our own, any more than what we possess is our own. We did not make ourselves; we cannot be supreme over ourselves. We cannot be our own masters. We are God's property by creation, by redemption, by regeneration. He has a triple claim upon us. Is it not our happiness thus to view the matter? Is it any happiness, or any comfort, to consider that we *are* our own? It may be thought so by the young and prosperous. These may think it a great thing to have everything, as they suppose, their own way— to depend on no one—to have to think of nothing out of sight—to be without the irksomeness of continual acknowledgment, continual prayer, continual reference of what they do to the will of another. But as time goes on, they, as all men, will find that independence was not made for man— that it is an unnatural state—may do for a while, but will not carry us on safely to the end. No, we are creatures; and, as being such, we have two duties, to be resigned and to be thankful.

Let us then view God's providences towards us more religiously than we have hitherto done. Let us try to gain a truer view of what we are, and where we are, in His kingdom. Let us humbly and reverently attempt to trace His guiding hand in the years which we have hitherto lived. Let us thankfully commemorate the many mercies He has vouchsafed to us in time past, the many sins He has not

[1] Job. i. 21.

remembered, the many dangers He has averted, the many prayers He has answered, the many mistakes He has corrected, the many warnings, the many lessons, the much light, the abounding comfort which He has from time to time given. Let us dwell upon times and seasons, times of trouble, times of joy, times of trial, times of refreshment. How did He cherish us as children! How did He guide us in that dangerous time when the mind began to think for itself, and the heart to open to the world! How did He with His sweet discipline restrain our passions, mortify our hopes, calm our fears, enliven our heavinesses, sweeten our desolateness, and strengthen our infirmities! How did He gently guide us towards the strait gate! How did He allure us along His everlasting way, in spite of its strictness, in spite of its loneliness, in spite of the dim twilight in which it lay! He has been all things to us. He has been, as He was to Abraham, Isaac, and Jacob, our God, our shield, and great reward, promising and performing, day by day. 'Hitherto hath He helped us.' 'He hath been mindful of us, and He will bless us.' He has not made us for nought; He has brought us thus far, in order to bring us further, in order to bring us on to the end. He will never leave us nor forsake us; so that we may boldly say, 'The Lord is my Helper; I will not fear what flesh can do unto me.' We may 'cast all our care upon Him, who careth for us.' What is it to us how our future path lies, if it be but His path? What is it to us whither it leads us, so that in the end it leads to Him? What is it to us what He puts upon us, so that He enables us to undergo it with a pure conscience, a true heart, not desiring anything of this world in comparison of Him? What is it to us what terror befalls us, if He be but at hand to protect and strengthen us? 'Thou, Israel,' He says, 'art My servant Jacob, whom I have chosen, the seed of

Abraham My friend.' 'Fear not, thou worm Jacob, and ye men of Israel; I will help thee, saith the Lord, and thy Redeemer, the Holy One of Israel.'

> Thus saith the Lord that created thee, O Jacob, and He that formed thee, O Israel, Fear not; for I have redeemed thee, I have called thee by thy name; thou art Mine. When thou passest through the waters, I will be with thee; and through the rivers, they shall not overflow thee; when thou walkest through the fire, thou shalt not be burned; neither shall the flame kindle upon thee. For I am the Lord thy God, the Holy One of Israel, thy Saviour.[1]*

[1] Isa. xli. 8, 14; xliii. 1–3.

*'Remembrance of past Mercies', *PPS*, V, Sermon 6.

## 8. THE HIDDEN PRESENCE
## OF CHRIST

---

## CHRIST HIDDEN FROM THE
## WORLD

*JOHN I. 5*
*'The light shineth in darkness, and the darkness comprehended it not.'*

OF all the thoughts which rise in the mind when contemplating the sojourn of our Lord Jesus Christ upon
earth,[1] none perhaps is more affecting and subduing than
the obscurity which attended it. I do not mean His obscure
condition, in the sense of its being humble; but the obscurity
in which He was shrouded, and the secrecy which He
observed. This characteristic of His first Advent is referred
to very frequently in Scripture, as in the text, 'The light
shineth in darkness, and the darkness comprehended it
not'; and is in contrast with what is foretold about His
second Advent. Then 'every eye shall see Him'; which
implies that all shall recognize Him; whereas, when He
came for the first time, though many saw Him, few indeed
discerned Him. It had been prophesied, 'When we shall see
Him there is no beauty that we should desire Him'; and
at the very end of His ministry He said to one of His twelve
chosen friends, 'Have I been so long time with you, and yet
hast thou not known Me, Philip?'[2]

---

[1] Preached on Christmas Day.
[2] Isa. liii. 2; John xiv. 9.

I propose to set before you one or two thoughts which arise from this very solemn circumstance, and which may, through God's blessing, be profitable.

1. And first, let us review some of the circumstances which marked His sojourn when on earth.

His condescension in coming down from heaven, in leaving His Father's glory and taking flesh, is so far beyond power of words or thought, that one might consider at first sight that it mattered little whether He came as a prince or a beggar. And yet after all, it *is* much more wonderful that He came in low estate, for this reason; because it might have been thought beforehand, that, though He condescended to come on earth, yet He would not submit to be overlooked and despised: now the rich are not despised by the world, and the poor are. If He had come as a great prince or noble, the world without knowing a whit more than He was God, yet would at least have looked up to Him and honoured Him, as being a prince; but when He came in a low estate, He took upon Him one additional humiliation, *contempt*—being contemned, scorned, rudely passed by, roughly profaned by His creatures.

What were the actual circumstances of His coming? His Mother is a poor woman; she comes to Bethlehem to be taxed, travelling, when her choice would have been to remain at home. She finds there is no room in the inn; she is obliged to betake herself to a stable; she brings forth her firstborn Son, and lays Him in a manger. That little babe, so born, so placed, is none other than the Creator of heaven and earth, the Eternal Son of God.

Well, he was born of a poor woman, laid in a manger, brought up to a lowly trade, that of a carpenter; and when He began to preach the Gospel He had not a place to lay His head: lastly, He was put to death, to an infamous and odious death, the death which criminals then suffered.

For the three last years of His life He preached the Gospel, I say, as we read in Scripture; but He did not begin to do so till He was thirty years old. For the first thirty years of His life He seems to have lived just as a poor man would live now. Day after day, season after season, winter and summer, one year and then another, passed on, as might happen to any of us. He passed from being a babe in arms to being a child, and then He became a boy, and so He grew up 'like a tender plant', increasing in wisdom and stature; and then He seems to have followed the trade of Joseph, his reputed father; going on in an ordinary way without any great occurrence, till He was thirty years old. How very wonderful is all this! that He should live here, doing nothing great, so long; living here, as if for the sake of living; not preaching, or collecting disciples, or apparently in any way furthering the cause which brought Him down from heaven. Doubtless there were deep and wise reasons in God's counsels for His going on so long in obscurity; I only mean that *we* do not know them.

And it is remarkable that those who were about Him seem to have treated Him as one of their equals. His brethren, that is, His near relations, His cousins, did not believe in Him. And it is very observable, too, that when He began to preach and a multitude collected, we are told, 'When His friends heard of it they went out to lay hold on Him; for they said, He is beside Himself.'[1] They treated Him as we might be disposed, and rightly, to treat any ordinary person now, who began to preach in the streets. I say 'rightly', because such persons generally preach a *new* Gospel, and therefore must be wrong. Also, they preach without being sent, and against authority; all which is

[1] Mark iii. 21.

wrong, too. Accordingly we are often tempted to say that
such people are 'beside themselves', or mad, and not un-
justly. It is often charitable to say so, for it is better to be
mad than to be disobedient. Well, what we should say of
such persons, this is what our Lord's friends said of Him.
They had lived so long with Him, and yet did not know
Him; did not understand what He was. They saw nothing
to mark a difference between Him and them. He was
dressed as others, He ate and drank as others, He came in
and went out, and spoke, and walked, and slept, as others.
He was in all respects a man, except that He did not sin;
and this great difference the many would not detect, because none of us understands those who are much better
than himself: so that Christ, the sinless Son of God, might
be living close to us, and we not discover it.

2. I say that Christ, the sinless Son of God, might be
living now in the world as our next-door neighbour, and
perhaps we not find it out. And this is a thought that should
be dwelt on. I do not mean to say that there are not a
number of persons who we could be sure were not Christ;
of course, no persons who lead bad and irreligious lives.
But there are a number of persons who are in no sense
irreligious or open to serious blame, who are very much
like each other at first sight, yet in God's eyes are very
different. I mean the great mass of what are called respectable men, who vary very much: some are merely decent
and outwardly correct persons, and have no great sense of
religion, do not deny themselves, have no ardent love of
God, but love the world; and, whereas their interest lies in
being regular and orderly, or they have no strong passions,
or have early got into the way of being regular, and their
habits are formed accordingly, they are what they are,
decent and correct, but very little more. But there are others

who look just the same to the world, who in their hearts are
very different; they make no great show, they go on in the
same quiet ordinary way as the others, but really they are
training to be saints in Heaven. They do all they can to
change themselves, to become like God, to obey God, to
discipline themselves, to renounce the world; but they do it
in secret, both because God tells them so to do and because
they do not like it to be known. Moreover, there are a number
of others between these two with more or less of worldliness
and more or less of faith. Yet they all look about the same,
to common eyes, because true religion is a hidden life in
the heart; and though it cannot exist without deeds, yet
these are for the most part secret deeds, secret charities,
secret prayers, secret self-denials, secret struggles, secret
victories.

Of course, in proportion as persons are brought out into
public life, they will be seen and scrutinized, and (in a
certain sense) known more; but I am talking of the ordinary
condition of people in private life, such as our Saviour was
for thirty years; and these look very like each other. And
there are so many of them that unless we get very near
them we cannot see any distinction between one and
another; we have no means to do so, and it is no business of
ours. And yet, though we have no right to judge others, but
must leave this to God, it is very certain that a really holy
man, a true saint, though he looks like other men, still has
a sort of secret power in him to attract others to him who
are like-minded, and to influence all who have anything in
them like him. And thus it often becomes a test, whether we
are like-minded with the Saints of God, whether they have
influence over us. And though we have seldom means of
knowing at the time who are God's own Saints, yet after all
is over we have; and then on looking back on what is past,

perhaps after they are dead and gone, if we knew them, we may ask ourselves what power they had over us, whether they attracted us, influenced us, humbled us, whether they made our hearts burn within us. Alas! too often we shall find that we were close to them for a long time, had means of knowing them, and knew them not; and that is a heavy condemnation on us, indeed. Now this was singularly exemplified in our Saviour's history, by how much He was so very holy. The holier a man is, the less he is understood by men of the world. All who have any spark of living faith will understand him in a measure, and the holier he is, they will, for the most part, be attracted the more; but those who serve the world will be blind to him, or scorn and dislike him, the holier he is. This, I say, happened to our Lord. He was All-holy, but 'the light shined in darkness, and the darkness comprehended it not'. His near relations did not believe in Him. And if this was really so, and for the reason I have said, it surely becomes a question whether we should have understood Him better than they: whether though He had been our next-door neighbour, or one of our family, we should have distinguished Him from anyone else, who was correct and quiet in his deportment; or rather, whether we should not, though we respected Him (alas, what a word! what language towards the Most High God!), yet even if we went as far as this, whether we should not have thought Him strange, eccentric, extravagant, and fanciful. Much less should we have detected any sparks of that glory which He had with the Father before the world was, and which was merely hidden not quenched by His earthly tabernacle. This, truly, is a very awful thought; because if He were near us for any long time, and we did not see anything wonderful in Him, we might take it as a clear proof that we were not His, for 'His sheep know His voice, and follow Him'; we might take it as a clear proof that we should not know Him, or admire His greatness, or adore His glory, or love His excellency, if we were admitted to His presence in heaven.

3. And here we are brought to another most serious thought, which I will touch upon. We are very apt to wish we had been born in the days of Christ, and in this way we excuse our misconduct, when conscience reproaches us. We say that had we had the advantage of being with Christ we should have had stronger motives, stronger restraints against sin. I answer, that so far from our sinful habits being reformed by the presence of Christ, the chance is that those same habits would have hindered us from recognizing Him. We should not have known He was present; and if He had even told us who He was we should not have believed Him. Nay, had we seen His miracles (incredible as it may seem), even they would not have made any lasting impression on us. Without going into this subject, consider only the possibility of Christ being close to us, even though He did no miracle, and our not knowing it; yet I believe this literally would have been the case with most men. But enough on this subject. What I am coming to is this: I wish you to observe what a fearful light this casts upon our prospects in the next world. We think heaven must be a place of happiness to us, if we do but get there; but the great probability is, if we can judge by what goes on here below, that a bad man, if brought to heaven, would not know he was in heaven; I do not go to the further question, whether, on the contrary, the very fact of his being in heaven with all his unholiness upon him, would not be a literal torment to him, and light up the fires of hell within him. This indeed would be a most dreadful way of finding out where he was. But let us suppose the lighter case: let us suppose he could

remain in heaven unblasted, yet it would seem that at least he would not know that he was there. He would see nothing wonderful there. Could men come nearer to God than when they seized Him, struck Him, spit on Him, hurried Him along, stripped Him, stretched out His limbs upon the cross, nailed Him to it, raised it up, stood gazing on Him, jeered Him, gave Him vinegar, looked close whether He was dead, and then pierced Him with a spear? O dreadful thought, that the nearest approaches man has made to God upon earth have been in blasphemy! Whether of the two came closer to Him, St. Thomas, who was allowed to reach forth his hand and reverently touch His wounds, and St. John, who rested on His bosom, or the brutal soldiers who profaned Him limb by limb, and tortured Him nerve by nerve? His Blessed Mother, indeed, came closer still to Him; and we, if we be true believers, still closer, who have them really, though spiritually, within us; but this is another, an inward sort of approach. Of those who approached Him externally, they came nearest, who knew nothing about it. So it is with sinners: they would walk close to the throne of God; they would stupidly gaze at it; they would touch it; they would meddle with the holiest things; they would go on intruding and prying, not meaning anything wrong by it, but with a sort of brute curiosity, till the avenging lightnings destroyed them; all because they have no *senses* to guide them in the matter. Our bodily senses tell us of the approach of good or evil on earth. By sound, by scent, by feeling we know what is happening to us. We know when we are exposing ourselves to the weather, when we are exerting ourselves too much. We have warnings, and feel we must not neglect them. Now, sinners have no spiritual senses; they can presage nothing; they do not know what is going to happen the next moment to them. So they go fearlessly further and further among precipices, till on a sudden they fall, or are smitten and perish. Miserable beings! and this is what sin does for immortal souls; that they should be like the cattle which are slaughtered at the shambles, yet touch and smell the very weapons which are to destroy them!

4. But, you may say, how does this concern us? Christ is not here; *we* cannot thus or in any less way insult His Majesty. Are we so sure of this? Certainly we cannot commit such open blasphemy; but it is another matter whether we cannot commit as great. For often sins are greater which are less startling; insults more bitter, which are not so loud; and evils deeper, which are more subtle. Do we not recollect a very awful passage? 'Whosoever speaketh a word against the Son of man, it shall be forgiven him; but whosoever speaketh against the Holy Ghost, it shall not be forgiven him.'[1] Now, I am not deciding whether or no his denunciation can be fulfilled in the case of Christians now, though when we recollect that we *are* at present under the ministration of that very Spirit of whom our Saviour speaks, this is a very serious question; but I quote it to show that there may be sins greater even than insult and injury offered to Christ's Person, though we should think that impossible, and though they could not be so flagrant or open. With this thought let it be considered:

First, that Christ is still on earth. He said expressly that He would come again. The Holy Ghost's coming is so really His coming that we might as well say that He was not here in the days of His flesh, when He was visibly in this world, as deny that He is here now, when He is here by His Divine Spirit. This indeed is a mystery, how God the Son and God the Holy Ghost, two Persons, can be one, how He

[1] Matt. xii. 32.

can be in the Spirit and the Spirit in Him; but so it is.

Next, if He is still on earth, yet is not visible (which cannot be denied), it is plain that He keeps Himself still in the condition which He chose in the days of His flesh. I mean, He is a hidden Saviour, and may be approached (unless we are careful) without due reverence and fear. I say, wherever He is (for that is a further question), still He is here, and again He is secret; and whatever be the tokens of His Presence, still they must be of a nature to admit of persons doubting where it is; and if they will argue, and be sharpwitted and subtle, they may perplex themselves and others, as the Jews did even in the days of His flesh, till He seems to them nowhere present on earth now. And when they come to think Him far away, of course they *feel* it to be impossible so to insult Him as the Jews did of old; and if nevertheless He *is* here, they *are* perchance approaching and insulting Him, though they so feel. And this was just the case of the Jews, for they too were ignorant what they were doing. It is probable, then, that we can now commit at least as great blasphemy towards Him as the Jews did first, because we are under the dispensation of that Holy Spirit, against whom even more heinous sins *can* be committed; next, because His presence now as little witnesses of itself, or is impressive to the many, as His bodily presence formerly.

We see a further reason for this apprehension, when we consider what the tokens of His presence now are; for they will be found to be of a nature easily to lead men into irreverence, unless they be humble and watchful. For instance, the Church is called 'His Body': what His material Body was when He was visible on earth, such is the Church now. It is the instrument of His Divine power; it is that which we must approach, to gain good from Him; it is that which by insulting we awaken His anger. Now, what is the Church but, as it were, a body of humiliation, almost provoking insult and profaneness, when men do not live by faith? An earthen vessel, far more so even than His body of flesh, for that was at least pure from all sin, and the Church is defiled in all her members. We know that her ministers at best are but imperfect and erring, and of like passions with their brethren; yet of them He has said, speaking not to the Apostles merely but to all the seventy disciples (to whom Christian ministers are in office surely equal), 'He that heareth you, heareth Me, and He that despiseth you despiseth Me, and he that despiseth Me, despiseth Him that sent Me.'

Again: He has made the poor, weak, and afflicted, tokens and instruments of His Presence; and here again, as is plain, the same temptation meets us to neglect or profane it. What He was, such are His chosen followers in this world; and as His obscure and defenceless state led men to insult and ill-treat Him, so the like peculiarities, in the tokens of His Presence, lead men to insult Him now. That such are His tokens is plain from many passages of Scripture: for instance, He says of children, 'Whoso shall receive one such little child in My Name, receiveth Me.' Again: He said to Saul, who was persecuting His followers, 'Why persecutest thou Me?' And He forewarns us that at the Last Day He will say to the righteous, 'I was an hungered, and ye gave Me meat; I was thirsty, and ye gave Me drink; I was a stranger, and ye took Me in; naked, and ye clothed Me; I was sick and ye visited Me; I was in prison, and ye came unto Me.' And He adds, 'Inasmuch as ye have done it unto the least of these My brethren, ye have done it unto Me.'[1] He observes the same connexion between

---

[1] Matt. xviii. 5; Acts ix. 4; Matt. xxv. 35–40.

Himself and His followers in His words to the wicked. What makes this passage the more awful and apposite, is this, which has been before now remarked,[1] that neither righteous nor wicked *knew* what they had done; even the righteous are represented as unaware that they had approached Christ. They say, 'Lord, *when* saw we Thee an hungered, and fed Thee, or thirsty, and gave Thee drink?' In every age, then, Christ is both in the world, and yet not publicly so more than in the days of His flesh.

And a similar remark applies to His Ordinances, which are at once most simple, yet most intimately connected with Him. St. Paul, in his First Epistle to the Corinthians, shows both how easy and how fearful it is to profane the Lord's Supper, while he states how great the excess of the Corinthians had been, yet also that it was a want of '*discerning* the Lord's Body'. When He was born into the world, the world knew it not. He was laid in a rude manger, among the cattle, but 'all the Angels of God worshipped Him'. Now, too, He is present upon a table, homely perhaps in make, and dishonoured in its circumstances; and faith adores, but the world passes by.

Let us then pray Him ever to enlighten the eyes of our understanding, that we may belong to the Heavenly Host, not to this world. As the carnal-minded would not perceive Him even in Heaven, so the spiritual heart may approach Him, possess Him, see Him, even upon earth.*

[1] *Vide* Pascal's *Pensées*.

*'Christ Hidden from the World', *PPS*, IV, Sermon 16.

# 9. THE MEANING OF EXISTENCE

## THE GREATNESS AND LITTLE-NESS OF HUMAN LIFE

### GEN. XLVII. 9

*'The days of the years of my pilgrimage are an hundred and thirty years: few and evil have the days of the years of my life been; and have not attained unto the days of the years of the life of my fathers, in the days of their pilgrimage.'*

WHY did the aged Patriarch call his days few, who had lived twice as long as men now live, when he spoke? Why did he call them evil, seeing he had on the whole lived in riches and honour, and, what is more, in God's favour? Yet he described his time as short, his days as evil, and his life as but a pilgrimage. Or if we allow that his afflictions were such as to make him reasonably think cheaply of his life, in spite of the blessings which attended it, yet that he should call it short, considering he had so much more time for the highest purposes of his being than we have, is at first sight surprising. He alludes indeed to the longer life which had been granted to his fathers, and perhaps felt a decrepitude greater than theirs had been; yet this difference between him and them could hardly be the real ground of his complaint in the text, or more than a confirmation or occasion of it. It was not because Abraham had lived one hundred and seventy-five years, and Isaac one hundred and eighty, and he himself, whose life was not yet finished, but one hundred and thirty, that he made this mournful speech. For it matters not, when time is gone, what length it has been; and this doubtless was the real cause why the Patriarch spoke as he did, not because his life was shorter than his fathers', but because it was well-nigh over. When life is past, it is all one whether it has lasted two hundred years or fifty. And it is this characteristic, stamped on human life in the days of its birth, viz. that it is mortal, which makes it under all circumstances and in every form equally feeble and despicable. All the points in which men differ, health and strength, high or low estate, happiness or misery, vanish before this common lot, mortality. Pass a few years, and the longest-lived will be gone; nor will what is past profit him then, except in its consequences.

And this sense of the nothingness of life, impressed on us by the very fact that it comes to an end, is much deepened when we contrast it with the capabilities of us who live it. Had Jacob lived Methuselah's age, he would have called it short. This is what we all feel, though at first sight it seems a contradiction, that even though the days as they go be slow, and be laden with many events, or with sorrows or dreariness, lengthening them out and making them tedious, yet the year passes quick though the hours tarry, and time bygone is as a dream, though we thought it would never go while it was going. And the reason seems to be this; that, when we contemplate human life in itself, in however small a portion of it, we see implied in it the presence of a soul, the energy of a spiritual existence, of an accountable being; consciousness tells us this concerning it every moment. But when we look back on it in memory, we view it, but externally, as a mere lapse of time, as a mere earthly history. And the longest duration of this external world is as dust and weighs nothing, against one moment's life of the world within. Thus we are ever expecting great things from life, from our internal consciousness every moment of our having souls; and we are ever being disappointed, on considering what we have gained from time past, or can hope from time to come. And life is ever promising and never fulfilling; and hence, however long it be, our days are few and evil. This is the particular view of the subject on which I shall now dwell.

Our earthly life then gives promise of what it does not accomplish. It promises immortality, yet it is mortal; it contains life in death and eternity in time; and it attracts us by beginnings which faith alone brings to an end. I mean, when we take into account the powers with which our souls are gifted as Christians, the very consciousness of these fills us with a certainty that they must last beyond this life; that is in the case of good and holy men, whose present state I say, is to them who know them well, an earnest of immortality. The greatness of their gifts, contrasted with their scanty time for exercising them, forces the mind forward to the thought of another life, as almost the necessary counterpart and consequence of this life, and certainly implied in this life, provided there be a righteous Governor of the world who does not make man for nought.

This is a thought which will come upon us not always, but under circumstances. And many perhaps of those who at first hearing may think they never felt it, may recognize what I mean, while I describe it.

I mean, when one sees some excellent person, whose graces we know, whose kindliness, affectionateness, tenderness, and generosity—when we see him dying (let him have lived ever so long; I am not supposing a premature death; let him live out his days), the thought is forced upon us with a sort of surprise: 'Surely, he is not to die yet; he has not yet had any opportunity of exercising duly those excellent gifts with which God has endowed him.' Let him have lived seventy or eighty years, yet it seems as if he had done nothing at all, and his life were scarcely begun. He has lived all his days perhaps in a private sphere; he has been engaged on a number of petty matters which died with the day, and yielded no apparent fruit. He has had just enough of trial under various circumstances to evidence, but not adequately to employ, what was in him. He has, we perhaps perceive, a noble benevolence of mind, a warmth of heart, and a beneficent temper, which, had it the means, would scatter blessings on every side; yet he has never been rich— he dies poor. We have been accustomed to say to ourselves, 'What would such a one be were he wealthy?' not as fancying he ever *will* have riches, but from feeling how he would become them; yet, when he actually does die as he lived, without them, we feel somehow disappointed—there has been a failure—his mind, we think, has never reached its scope—he has had a treasure within him which has never been used. His days have been but few and evil, and have become old unseasonably, compared with his capabilities; and we are driven by a sense of these, to look on to a future state as a time when they will be brought out and come into effect. I am not attempting by such reflections to prove that there is a future state; let us take that for granted. I mean, over and above our positive belief in this great truth, we are actually driven to a belief, we attain a sort of sensible conviction of that life to come, a certainty striking home to our hearts and piercing them, by this imperfection in what is present. The very greatness of our powers makes this life look pitiful; the very pitifulness of this life forces on our thoughts to another; and the prospect of another gives a dignity and value to this life which promises it; and thus this life is at once great and little, and we rightly contemn it while we exalt its importance.

And, if this life is short, even when longest, from the great disproportion between it and the powers of regenerate man, still more is this the case, of course, where it is cut short, and death comes prematurely. Men there are, who, in a single moment of their lives, have shown a superhuman height and majesty of mind which it would take ages for them to employ on its proper objects, and, as it were, to exhaust; and who by such passing flashes, like rays of the sun, and the darting of lightning, give token of their immortality, give token to us that they are but Angels in disguise, the elect of God sealed for eternal life, and destined to judge the world and to reign with Christ for ever. Yet they are suddenly taken away, and we have hardly recognized them when we lose them. Can we believe that they are not removed for higher things elsewhere? This is sometimes said with reference to our intellectual powers; but it is still more true of our moral nature. There is something in moral truth and goodness, in faith, in firmness, in heavenly-mindedness, in meekness, in courage, in loving-kindness, to which this world's circumstances are quite unequal, for which the longest life is insufficient, which makes the highest opportunities of this world disappointing, which must burst the prison of this world to have its appropriate range. So that when a good man dies, one is led to say, 'He has not half showed himself, he has had nothing to exercise him; his days are gone like a shadow, and he is withered like grass.'

I say the word 'disappointing' is the only word to express our feelings on the death of God's saints. Unless our faith be very active, so as to pierce beyond the grave, and realize the future, we feel depressed at what seems like a failure of great things. And from this very feeling surely, by a sort of contradiction, we may fairly take hope; for if this life be so disappointing, so unfinished, surely it is not the whole. This feeling of disappointment will often come upon us in an especial way, on happening to hear of or to witness the deathbeds of holy men. The hour of death seems to be a season, of which, in the hands of Providence, much might be *made*, if I may use the term; much might be done for the glory of God, the good of man, and the manifestation of the person dying. And beforehand friends will perhaps look forward, and expect that great things are then to take place, which they shall never forget. Yet, 'how dieth the wise man? as the fool.'[1] Such is the preacher's experience, and our own bears witness to it. King Josiah, the zealous servant of the Living God, died the death of wicked Ahab, the worshipper of Baal. True Christians die as other men. One dies by a sudden accident, another in battle, another without friends to see how he dies, a fourth is insensible or not himself. Thus the opportunity seems thrown away, and we are forcibly reminded that 'the manifestation of the sons of God'[2] is hereafter; that 'the earnest expectation of the creature' is but waiting for it; that this life is unequal to the burden of so great an office as the due exhibition of those secret ones who shall one day 'shine forth as the sun in the kingdom of their Father'.[3]

But further (if it be allowable to speculate), one can even conceive the same kind of feeling, and a most transporting one, to come over the soul of the faithful Christian, when just separated from the body, and conscious that his trial is once for all over. Though his life has been a long and painful discipline, yet when it is over, we may suppose him to feel

[1] Eccles. ii. 16.
[2] Rom. viii. 19.
[3] Matt. xiii. 43.

at the moment the same sort of surprise at its being ended, as generally follows any exertion in this life, when the object is gained and the anticipation over. When we have wound up our minds for any point of time, any great event, an interview with strangers, or the sight of some wonder, or the occasion of some unusual trial, when it comes, and is gone, we have a strange reverse of feeling from our changed circumstances. Such, but without any mixture of pain, without any lassitude, dullness, or disappointment, may be the happy contemplation of the disembodied spirit; as if it said to itself,

> So all is now over; this is what I have so long waited for; for which I have nerved myself; against which I have prepared, fasted, prayed, and wrought righteousness. Death is come and gone—it is over. Ah! is it possible? What an easy trial, what a cheap price for eternal glory! A few sharp sicknesses, or some acute pain awhile, or some few and evil years, or some struggles of mind, dreary desolateness for a season, fightings and fears, afflicting bereavements, or the scorn and ill-usage of the world —how they fretted me, how much I thought of them, yet how little really they are! How contemptible a thing is human life— contemptible in itself, yet in its effects invaluable! for it has been to me like a small seed of easy purchase, germinating and ripening into bliss everlasting.

Such being the unprofitableness of this life, viewed in itself, it is plain how we should regard it while we go through it. We should remember that it is scarcely more than an accident of our being—that it is no part of ourselves, who are immortal; that we are immortal spirits, independent of time and space, and that this life is but a sort of outward stage, on which we act for a time, and which is only sufficient and only intended to answer the purpose of trying whether we will serve God or no. We should consider ourselves to be in this world in no fuller sense than players in any game are in the game; and life to be a sort of dream, as detached and as different from our real eternal existence as a dream differs from waking; a serious dream, indeed, as affording a means of judging us, yet in itself a kind of shadow without substance, a scene set before us, in which we seem to be, and in which it is our duty to act just as if all we saw had a truth and reality, because all that meets us influences us and our destiny. The regenerate soul is taken into communion with Saints and Angels, and its 'life is hid with Christ in God';[1] it has a place in God's court, and is not of this world—looking into this world as a spectator might look at some show or pageant, except when called from time to time to take a part. And while it obeys the instinct of the senses, it does so for God's sake, and it submits itself to things of time so far as to be brought to perfection by them, that, when the veil is withdrawn and it sees itself to be, where it ever has been, in God's kingdom, it may be found worthy to enjoy it. It is this view of life which removes from us all surprise and disappointment that it is so incomplete: as well might we expect any chance event which happens in the course of it to be complete, any casual conversation with a stranger, or the toil or amusement of an hour.

Let us then thus account of our present state: it is precious as revealing to us, amid shadows and figures, the existence and attributes of Almighty God and His elect people: it is precious, because it enables us to hold intercourse with immortal souls who are on their trial as we are. It is momentous, as being the scene and means of our trial; but beyond this it has no claims upon us. 'Vanity of vanities, says the Preacher, all is vanity.' We may be poor or rich,

[1] Col. iii. 3.

young or old, honoured or slighted, and it ought to affect us no more, neither to elate us nor depress us, than if we were actors in a play, who know that the characters they represent are not their own, and that though they may appear to be superior one to another, to be kings or to be peasants, they are in reality all on a level. The one desire which should move us should be, first of all, that of seeing Him face to face, who is now hid from us; and next of enjoying eternal and direct communication, in and through Him, with our friends around us, whom at present we know only through the medium of sense, by precarious and partial channels, which give us little insight into their hearts.

These are suitable feelings towards this attractive but deceitful world. What have we to do with its gifts and honours, who, having been already baptized into the world to come, are no longer citizens of this? Why should we be anxious for a long life, or wealth, or credit, or comfort, who know that the next world will be everything which our hearts can wish, and that not in appearance only, but truly and everlastingly? Why should we rest in this world, when it is the token and promise of another? Why should we be content with its surface, instead of appropriating what is stored beneath it? To those who live by faith, everything they see speaks of that future world; the very glories of nature, the sun, moon, and stars, and the richness and the beauty of the earth, are as types and figures witnessing and teaching the invisible things of God. All that we see is destined one day to burst forth into a heavenly bloom, and to be transfigured into immortal glory. Heaven at present is out of sight, but in due time, as snow melts and discovers what it lay upon, so will this visible creation fade away before those greater splendours which are behind it, and on which at present it depends. In that day shadows will

retire, and the substance show itself. The sun will grow pale
and be lost in the sky, but it will be before the radiance of
Him whom it does but image, the Sun of Righteousness,
with healing on His wings, who will come forth in visible
form, as a bridegroom out of his chamber, while His perishable type decays. The stars which surround it will be re-
placed by Saints and Angels circling His throne. Above and
below, the clouds of the air, the trees of the field, the waters
of the great deep will be found impregnated with the forms
of everlasting spirits, the servants of God which do His
pleasure. And our own mortal bodies will then be found in
like manner to contain within them an inner man, which
will then receive its due proportions, as the soul's harmoni-
ous organ, instead of that gross mass of flesh and blood
which sight and touch are sensible of. For this glorious
manifestation the whole creation is at present in travail,
earnestly desiring that it may be accomplished in its
season.

These are thoughts to make us eagerly and devoutly
say, 'Come, Lord Jesus, to end the time of waiting, of darkness, of turbulence, of disputing, of sorrow, of care.' These
are thoughts to lead us to rejoice in every day and hour that
passes, as bringing us nearer the time of His appearing, and
the termination of sin and misery. They are thoughts which
ought thus to affect us; and so they would, were it not for
the load of guilt which weighs upon us, for sins committed
against light and grace. O that it were otherwise with us!
O that we were fitted duly to receive this lesson which the
world gives us, and had so improved the gifts of life, that
while we felt it to be perishing, we might rejoice in it as
precious! O that we were not conscious of deep stains upon
our souls, the accumulations of past years, and of infirmities
continually besetting us! Were it not for all this—were it

not for our unprepared state, as in one sense it may truly be called, how gladly should we hail each new month and year as a token that our Saviour is so much nearer to us than He ever has been yet! May He grant His grace abundantly to us, to make us meet for His presence, that we may not be ashamed before Him at His coming! May He vouchsafe to us the full grace of His ordinances: may He feed us with His choicest gifts: may He expel the poison from our souls: may He wash us clean in His precious blood, and give us the fullness of faith, love, and hope, as foretastes of the heavenly portion which He destines for us!*

*'The Greatness and Littleness of Human Life', *PPS*, IV, Sermon 14.

# 10. WAITING FOR CHRIST

---

## WAITING FOR CHRIST
### (ASCENSION)

*REV. XXII. 20*
*'He who testifieth these things, saith, Surely I come quickly. Amen. Even so, come, Lord Jesus.'*

WHEN our Lord was going away, He said He would quickly come again; yet knowing that by 'quickly' He did not mean what would be at first sight understood by the word, He added, 'suddenly', or 'as a thief'. 'Behold I come as a thief; blessed is he that watcheth, and keepeth his garments.'[1] Had His coming been soon, in our sense of the word, it could not well have been sudden. Servants who are bid to wait for their master's return from an entertainment, could not, one should think, be overtaken by that return. It was because to us His coming would not *seem* soon, that it *was* sudden. What you expect to come, you wait for; what fails to come, you give up; while, then, Christ said that His coming would be soon, yet by saying it would be sudden, He said that to us it would seem long.

Yet though to us He seems to delay, yet He has declared that His coming is speedy, He has bid us ever look out for His coming; and His first followers, as the Epistles show us, *were* ever looking out for it. Surely it is our duty to look out for it, as likely to come immediately, though hitherto for

[1] Rev. xvi. 15.

near two thousand years the Church has been looking out
in vain.

Is it not something significant that, in the last book of
Scripture, which more than any other implies a long con-
tinuance to the Christian Church—that there we should
have such express and repeated assurances that Christ's
coming would be speedy? Even in the last chapter we are
told it three times. 'Behold I come quickly; blessed is he
that keepeth the sayings of the prophecy of this book.'
'Behold I come quickly, and My reward is with Me.' And
again, in the text, 'He that testifieth these things, saith,
Surely I come quickly.' Such is the announcement; and, in
consequence, we are commanded to be ever looking out for
the great Day, to 'wait for His Son from heaven';[1] to 'look
and haste unto the coming of the day of God'.[2]

It is true, indeed, that in one place St. Paul cautions his
brethren against expecting the immediate coming of Christ;
but he does not say more than that Christ will send a sign
immediately before His coming—a certain dreadful enemy
of the truth—which is to be followed by Himself at once,
and therefore does not stand in our way, or prevent eager
eyes from looking out for Him. And, in truth, St. Paul seems
rather to be warning his brethren against being disappointed
if Christ did not come, than hindering them from expecting
Him.

Now it may be objected that this is a kind of paradox;
how is it possible, it may be asked, ever to be expecting
what has so long been delayed? What has been so long
coming, may be longer still. It was possible, indeed, for the
early Christians, who had no experience of the long period
which the Church was to remain on earth, to look out for

[1] 1 Thess. i. 10.
[2] 2 Pet. iii. 12.

Christ; but we cannot help using our reason: there are no more grounds to expect Christ now than at those many former times, when, as the event showed, He did not come. Christians have ever been expecting the last day, and ever meeting with disappointment. They have seen what they thought symptoms of His coming, and peculiarities in their own times, which a little more knowledge of the world, a more enlarged experience, would have shown them to be common to all times. They have ever been frightened without good reason, fretting in their narrow minds, and building on their superstitious fancies. What age of the world has there been in which people did not think the Day of Judgment coming? Such expectation has but evidenced and fostered indolence and superstition; it is to be considered as a mere weakness.

Now I shall attempt to say something in answer to this objection.

1. And first, considered as an objection to a habit of continual waiting (to use the common phrase), it proves too much. If it is consistently followed up, no age ought ever to expect the day of Christ; the age in which He shall come (whenever it is) ought not to expect Him; which is the very thing He has warned us against. He nowhere warns us against what is contemptuously called superstition; but He expressly warns us against high-minded security. If it be true that Christians have expected Him when He did not come, it is quite as true that when He does come, the world will not expect Him. If it be true that Christians have fancied signs of His coming, when there were none, it is equally true that the world will not see the signs of His coming when they are present. His signs are not so plain but you have to search for them; not so plain but you may be mistaken *in* your search; and your choice lies between the

risk of thinking you see what is not and of not seeing what
is. True it is, that many times, many ages, have Christians
been mistaken in thinking they discerned Christ's coming;
but better a thousand times think Him coming when He is
not than once think Him not coming when He is. Such is
the difference between Scripture and the world; judging by
Scripture, you would ever be expecting Christ; judging by
the world, you would never expect Him. Now He must come
one day, sooner or later. Worldly men have their scoff at
our failure of discernment now; but whose will be the want
of discernment, whose the triumph then? And what does
Christ think of their present scoff? He expressly warns us,
by His Apostle, of scoffers, who shall say,

> Where is the promise of His coming? for since the fathers fell
> asleep, all things continue as they were from the beginning of
> the creation. . . . But, beloved [continues St. Peter], be not
> ignorant of this one thing, that one day is with the Lord as a
> thousand years, and a thousand years as one day.[1]

It should be recollected, too, that the enemies of Christ
have ever been expecting the downfall of His religion, age
after age; and I do not see why the one expectation is more
unreasonable than the other; indeed they illustrate each
other. So it is, undeterred by the failure of former anticipations, unbelievers are ever expecting that the Church and
the religion of the Church are coming to an end. They
thought so in the last century. They think so now. They
ever think the light of truth is going out, and that their hour
of victory is come. Now, I repeat, I do not see why it is
reasonable to expect the overthrow of religion still, after so
many failures; and yet unreasonable, because of previous
disappointments, to expect the coming of Christ. Nay,

[1] 2 Pet. iii. 4, 8.

Christians at least, over and above the aspect of things, can point to an express promise of Christ, that He will one day come; whereas unbelievers, I suppose, do not profess any grounds at all for expecting their own triumph, except the signs of the times. They are sanguine, because they seem so strong, and the Church of God seems so weak; yet they have not enlarged their minds enough by the contemplation of past history to know that such apparent strength on the one side, and such apparent weakness on the other, has ever been the state of the world and the Church; and that this has ever been one chief or rather the main reason, why Christians have expected the immediate end of all things, because the prospects of religion *were* so gloomy. So that, in fact, Christians and unbelievers have taken precisely the same view of the facts of the case; only they have drawn distinct conclusions from them, according to their creed. The Christian has said, 'All looks so full of tumult, that the world is coming to an end'; and the unbeliever has said, 'All is so full of tumult, that the Church is coming to an end'; and there is nothing, surely, more superstitious in the one opinion than in the other.

Now when Christians and unbelievers thus unite in expecting substantially the same thing, though they view it differently, according to their respective modes of thought, there cannot be anything very extravagant in the expectation itself; there must be something ever present in the world which warrants it. And I hold this to be the case. Ever since Christianity came into the world, it has been, in one sense, going out of it. It is so uncongenial to the human mind, it is so spiritual, and man is so earthly, it is apparently so defenceless, and has so many strong enemies, so many false friends, that every age, as it comes, may be called 'the last time'. It has made great conquests, and done great works; but still it has done all, as the Apostle says of himself, 'in weakness, and in fear, and in much trembling'.[1] *How* it is that it is always failing, yet always continuing, God only knows who wills it—but so it is; and it is no paradox to say, on the one hand, that it has lasted eighteen hundred years, that it may last many years more, and yet that it draws to an end, nay, is likely to end any day. And God would have us give our minds and hearts to the latter side of the alternative, to open them to impressions *from* this side, viz. that the end is coming—it being a wholesome thing to live as if *that* will come in our day, which may come any day.

It was different during the ages before Christ came. The Saviour was to come. He was to bring perfection, and religion was to grow *towards* that perfection. There was a system of successive revelations going on, first one and then another; each prophet in his turn adding to the store of Divine truth, and gradually tending towards the full Gospel. Time was measured out for believing minds before Christ came, by the word of prophecy; so that He never could be expected in any age before the 'fullness of time' in which He came. The chosen people were not bidden to expect Him at once; but after a sojourning in Canaan, and a captivity in Egypt, and a wandering in the wilderness, and judges, and kings, and prophets, at length seventy long weeks were determined to introduce Him into the world. Thus His delay was, as I may say, *recognized* then; and, *during* His delay, other doctrines, other rules, were given to fill the interval. But when once the Christ had come, as the Son over His own house, and with His perfect Gospel, nothing remained but to gather in His saints. No higher Priest could come—no truer doctrine. The Light and Life

[1] 1 Cor. ii. 3.

R.–K

of men had appeared, and had suffered, and had risen again; and nothing more was left to do. Earth had had its most solemn event, and seen its most august sight; and therefore it was the last time. And hence, though time intervene between Christ's first and second coming, it is not *recognized* (as I may say) in the Gospel scheme, but is, as it were, an accident. For so it was, that up to Christ's coming in the flesh, the course of things ran straight towards that end, nearing it by every step; but now, under the Gospel, that course has (if I may so speak) altered its direction, as regards His second coming, and runs, not towards the end, but along it, and on the brink of it; and is at all times equally near that great event, which, did it run towards, it would at once run into. Christ, then, is ever at our doors; as near eighteen hundred years ago as now, and not nearer now than then; and not nearer when He comes than now. When He says that He will come soon, 'soon' is not a word of time, but of natural order. This present state of things, 'the present distress' as St. Paul calls it, is ever *close upon* the next world, and resolves itself into it. As when a man is given over, he may die any moment, yet lingers; as an implement of war may any moment explode, and must at some time; as we listen for a clock to strike, and at length it surprises us; as a crumbling arch hangs, we know not how, and is not safe to pass under; so creeps on this feeble weary world, and one day, before we know where we are, it will end.

And here I may observe in passing, on the light thus thrown upon the doctrine, that Christ is the sole Priest under the Gospel, or that the Apostles ever sit on twelve thrones, judging the twelve tribes of Israel, or that Christ is with them always, even unto the end of the world. Do you not see the force of these expressions? The Jewish

Covenant, indeed, had 'sundry times', which were ordered 'in divers manners'; it had a long array of priests and a various history; one part of the series holier than another, and nearer heaven. But when Christ had come, suffered, and ascended, He was henceforth ever near us, ever at hand, even though He was not actually returned, ever scarcely gone, ever all but come back. He is the only Ruler and Priest in His Church, dispensing gifts, and has appointed none to supersede Him, because He is departed only for a brief season. Aaron took the place of Christ, and had a priesthood of His own; but Christ's priests have no priesthood but His. They are merely His shadows and organs, they are His outward signs; and what they do, He does; when they baptize, He is baptizing; when they bless, He is blessing. He is in all acts of His Church, and one of its acts is not more truly His act than another, for all are His. Thus we are, in all times of the Gospel, brought close to His Cross. We stand, as it were, under it, and receive its blessings fresh from it; only that since, historically speaking, time has gone on, and the Holy One is away, certain outward forms are necessary, by way of bringing us again under His shadow; and we enjoy those blessings through a mystery, or sacramentally, in order to enjoy them really. All this witnesses to the duty both of remembering and of looking out for Christ, teaching us to neglect the present, to rely on no plans, to form no expectations, for the future, but so to live in faith, as if He had not left us, so in hope, as if He had returned to us. We must try to live as if the Apostles were living, and we must try to muse upon our Lord's life in the Gospels, not as a history, but as if a recollection.

2. This leads me to remark upon a second aspect under which the objection in question may be urged; viz. that this waiting for Christ is not only extravagant in its very

idea, but becomes a superstition and weakness whenever carried into effect. The mind, intent upon the thought of an awful visitation close at hand, begins to fancy signs of it in the natural and moral world, and mistakes the ordinary events of God's providence for miracles. Thus Christians are brought into bondage, and substitute for the Gospel a fond religion, in which imagination takes the place of faith, and things visible and earthly take the place of Scripture. This is the objection; yet the text, on the other hand, while it sanctions the expectation, in the words 'Surely I come quickly', surely sanctions the temper of waiting also, by adding, 'Amen, even so, come, Lord Jesus.'

I observe, then, that though Christians might be mistaken in what they took to be signs of Christ's coming, yet they were not wrong in their state of mind; they were not mistaken in looking out, and that for Christ. Whether credulous or not, they only acted as one acts towards some person beloved, or revered, or admired on earth. Consider the mode in which loyal persons look up to a good prince; you will find stories current, up and down the country, in his favour; people delight in believing that they have fallen in with tokens of his beneficence, nobleness, and paternal kindness. Many of these reports are false, yet others are true, and, on the whole, we should not think highly of that man who, instead of being touched at this mutual sympathy between sovereign and people, occupied himself merely in carping at what he called their credulity, and sifting the accuracy of this or that particular story. A great thing, truly, after all, to be able to detect a few mis-statements, and to expose a few fictions, and to be without a heart! And forsooth, on the other hand, a sad deficiency in that people, I suppose, merely to be right on the whole, not in every particular, and to have the heart right! Who would envy such a man's knowledge? Who would not rather have that people's ignorance? And, in like manner, I had rather be he, who, from love of Christ and want of science, thinks some strange sight in the sky, comet or meteor, to be the sign of His coming, than the man, who, from more knowledge and from lack of love, laughs at the mistake.

Before now, religious persons have taken appearances in the heaven for signs of Christ's coming, which do not now frighten us at all. Granted, but what then? Let us consider the state of the case. Of old time it was not *known* generally that certain heavenly bodies moved and appeared at *fixed* times and by a rule; now it is known; that is, now men are *accustomed* to see them, then they were not accustomed. We know as little now as then *how* they come, or why; but then men were startled when they saw them, because they were strange, and now they are not strange, and therefore men are not startled. But how was it therefore absurd and ridiculous (for so it is that persons nowadays talk), why was it a foolish fond thing in a man to be impressed by what was rare and strange? Take a parallel case: travelling is common now, it was not common formerly. In consequence, we now travel without any serious emotion at parting from our friends; but then, because it was uncommon, even when risks were the same and the absence as long, persons did not go from home without much preparation, many prayers, and much leave-taking. I do not see any thing very censurable in being more impressed at uncommon things than at common.

And you will observe, that in the case of which I am speaking, persons who are looking out for Christ are not only, *in that* they look out, acting in obedience to Him, but are looking out—in their very *way* of looking out, through the very signs through which they look out—in obedience to Him. Always since the first, Christians have been looking out for Christ *in* the signs of the natural and moral world. If they have been poor and uneducated, strange sights in the sky, or tremblings of the ground, storms, failure of harvest, or disease, or anything monstrous and unnatural, has made them think that He was at hand. If they were in a way to take a view of the social and political world, then the troubles of states—wars, revolutions, and the like—have been additional circumstances which served to impress them, and kept their hearts awake for Christ. Now all these are nothing else but those very things which He Himself has told us to dwell upon, and has given us as signs of His coming.

> There shall be signs [He says], in the sun, and in the moon, and in the stars; and upon the earth distress of nations, with perplexity, the sea and the waves roaring; men's hearts failing them for fear, and for looking after those things which are coming on the earth; for the powers of heaven shall be shaken. . . . And when these things begin to come to pass, then look up and lift up your heads, for your redemption draweth nigh.[1]

One day the lights of heaven *will* be signs; one day the affairs of nations also *will* be signs; why, then, is it superstitious to *look* towards them? It is not. We may be wrong in the particulars we rest upon, and may show our ignorance in doing so; but there is nothing ridiculous or contemptible in our ignorance, and there is much that is religious in our watching. It is better to be wrong in our watching, than not to watch at all.

Nor does it follow that Christians were wrong, even in their particular anticipations, though Christ did not come, whereas they said, they saw His signs. Perhaps they *were* His signs, and He withdrew them again. Is there no such

[1] Luke xxi. 25, 26, 28.

thing as countermanding? Do not skilful men in matters of this world sometimes form anticipations which turn out wrong, and yet we say that they *ought* to have been right? The sky threatens and then clears again. Or some military leader orders his men forward, and then for some reason recalls them; shall we say that informants were wrong who brought the news that he was moving? Well, in one sense Christ is ever moving forward, ever checking, the armies of heaven. Signs of the white horses are ever appearing, ever vanishing. 'Clouds return after the rain'; and His servants are not wrong in pointing to them, and saying that the weather is breaking, though it does not break, for it is ever unsettled.

And another thing should be observed, that though Christians have ever been expecting Christ, ever pointing to His signs, they have never said that He was come. They have but said that He was just coming, *all but* come. And so He was and is. Enthusiasts, sectaries, wild presumptuous men, *they* have said that He was *actually* come, or they have pointed out the exact year and day in which He would come. Not so His humble followers. They have neither announced nor sought Him, either in the desert or in the secret chambers, nor have they attempted to determine 'the times and seasons, which the Father has put in His own power'. They have but waited; when He actually comes, they will not mistake Him; and before then, they pronounce nothing. They do but see His forerunners.

Surely there can be no great harm, and nothing very ridiculous, where men are religious, in thus thinking the events of their day more than ordinary, in fancying that the world's matters are winding up, and that events are thickening for a final visitation; for, let it be observed, Scripture sanctions us in interpreting *all* that we see in the world in a

religious sense, and as if all things were tokens and revelations of Christ, His Providence, and will. I mean that if this
lower world, which seems to go on in its own way, indepen-
dently of Him, governed by fixed laws or swayed by lawless
hearts, will, nevertheless, one day in an awful way, herald
His coming to judge it, surely it is not impossible that the
same world, both in its physical order and its temporal
course, speaks of Him also in other manners. At first, indeed, one might argue that this world did but speak a language contrary to Him; that in Scripture it is described as
opposed to God, to truth, to faith, to heaven; that it is said
to be a deceitful veil, misrepresenting things, and keeping
the soul from God. How then, it may be asked, can this
world have upon it tokens of His presence, or bring us near
to Him? Yet certainly so it is, that in spite of the world's
evil, after all, He is in it and speaks through it, though not
loudly. When He came in the flesh 'He was in the world,
and the world was made by Him, and the world knew Him
not'. Nor did He strive nor cry, nor lift up His voice in the
streets. So it is now. He still is here; He still whispers to us,
He still makes signs to us. But His voice is so low, and the
world's din is so loud, and His signs are so covert, and the
world is so restless, that it is difficult to determine when He
addresses us, and what He says. Religious men cannot but
feel, in various ways, that His providence is guiding them
and blessing them personally, on the whole; yet when they
attempt to put their finger upon the times and places, the
traces of His presence disappear. Who is there, for instance,
but has been favoured with answers to prayer, such that,
at the time, he has felt he never could again be unbelieving?
Who has not had strange coincidences in his course of life
which brought before him, in an overpowering way, the
hand of God? Who has not had thoughts come upon him

with a sort of mysterious force, for his warning or his direction? And some persons, perhaps, experience stranger things still. Wonderful providences have before now been brought about by means of dreams; or in other still more unusual ways Almighty God has at time interposed. And then, again, things which come before our eyes, in such wise take the form of types and omens of things moral or future, that the spirit within us cannot but reach forward and presage what it is not told from what it sees. And sometimes these presages are remarkably fulfilled in the event. And then, again, the fortunes of men are so singularly various, as if a law of success and prosperity embraced a certain number, and a contrary law others. All this being so, and the vastness and mystery of the world being borne in upon us, we may well begin to think that there is nothing here below, but, for what we know, has a connexion with everything else; the most distant events may yet be united, the meanest and highest may be parts of one; and God may be teaching us and offering us knowledge of His ways, if we will but open our eyes, in all the ordinary matters of the day. This is what thoughtful persons come to believe, and they begin to have a sort of faith in the Divine meaning of the accidents (as they are called) of life, and a readiness to take impressions from them, which may easily become excessive, and which, whether excessive or not, is sure to be ridiculed by the world at large as superstition. Yet, considering Scripture tells us that the very hairs of our head are all numbered by God, that all things are ours, and that all things work together for our good, it does certainly encourage us in thus looking out for His presence in everything that happens, however trivial, and in holding that to religious ears even the bad world prophesies of Him.

Yet, I say, this religious waiting upon God through the

day, which is so like that spirit of watching which is under consideration, is just as open to objection and scoffing from the world. God does not so speak to us through the occurrences of life that you can persuade others that He speaks. He does not act upon such explicit laws that you can speak of them with certainty. He gives us sufficient tokens of Himself to raise our minds in awe towards Him; but He seems so frequently to undo what He has done, and to suffer counterfeits of His tokens, that a conviction of His wonder-working presence can but exist in the individual himself. It is not a truth that can be taught and recognized in the face of men; it is not of a nature to be urged upon the world at large, nay, even on religious persons, as a principle. God gives us enough to make us inquire and hope; not enough to make us insist and argue.

I have all along been speaking of thoughtful and conscientious persons; those who do their duty, and who study Scripture. It is quite certain that this regard to outward occurrences does become superstition, when it is found in men of irreligious lives, or of slender knowledge of Scripture. The great and chief revelation which God has made us of His will is through Christ and His Apostles. They have given us a knowledge of the truth; they have sent forth heavenly principles and doctrines into the world; they have accompanied that revealed truth by Divine sacraments, which convey to the heart what otherwise would be a mere outward and barren knowledge; and they have told us to practise what we know, and obey what we are taught, that the Word of Christ may be formed and dwell in us. They have been inspired, moreover, to write Holy Scriptures for our learning and comfort; and in those Scriptures we find the history of this world interpreted for us by a heavenly rule. When, then, a man, thus formed and fortified within, with these living principles in his heart, with this firm hold and sight of things invisible, with likings, opinions, views, aims, moulded upon God's revealed law, looks abroad into the world, he does not come to the world for a revelation—he has one already. He does not take his religion from the world, nor does he set an overvalue upon the tokens and presages which he sees there. But far different is the case when a man is not thus enlightened and informed by revealed truth. Then he is but a prey, he becomes the slave, of the occurrences and events, the sights and sounds, the omens and prodigies, which meet him in the world, natural and moral. His religion is a bondage to things perishable, and idolatry of the creature, and is, in the worst sense of the word, superstition. Hence it is a common remark that irreligious men are most open to superstition. For they have a misgiving that there is something great and Divine somewhere: and since they have it not within them, they have no difficulty in believing that it is anywhere else, wherever men pretend to the possession of it. Thus you find in history men in high place practising unlawful arts, consulting professed wizards, or giving heed to astrology. Others have had their lucky and unlucky days; others have been the sport of dreams, or of other idle fancies. And you have had others bowing themselves down to idols. For they have had no principle, no root in themselves. They have been ignorant, too, of Scripture, in which God has most mercifully removed the veil off a portion of this world's history, in order that we may see *how* He works. Scripture is the key by which we are given to interpret the world; but they who have it not, roam amid the shadows of the world, and interpret things at random.

The same want of inward religious principle is shown in the light, senseless way in which so many adopt wrong forms of religious profession. He who has the light of Christ within him, hears the voice of enthusiastic, mistaken, self-willed, or hypocritical men, calling him to follow them, without being moved. But when a man is conscious he is a wilful sinner, and not at peace with God, when his own heart is against him, and he has no principle, no stay within him, then he is the prey of the first person who comes to him with strong language, and bids him believe in him. Hence you find numbers running eagerly after men who profess to work miracles, or who denounce the Church as apostate, or who maintain that none are saved but those who agree with themselves, or anyone who, without any warrant of his being right, speaks confidently. Hence the multitude is so open to sudden alarms. You hear of their rushing out of a city in numbers at some idle prediction that the Day of Judgment is coming. Hence so many, in the private and lower ranks of life, are so full of small super-stitions, which are too minute to mention; all because they have not the light of truth burning in their heart.

But the true Christian is not of these. To him apply St. Paul's words, 'All things are lawful unto me, but all things are not expedient; all things are lawful for me, but I will not be brought under the power of any.'[1] He knows how to 'use this world as not abusing it'. He *depends* on nothing in this world. He trusts not *its* sights against the revealed Word. 'Thou wilt keep him in perfect peace whose mind is stayed on Thee, because he trusteth in Thee.' Such is the promise made to him. And if he looks out into the world to seek, it is not to seek what he does not know, but what he does. He does not seek a Lord and Saviour. He has 'found the Messias' long since; and he is looking out for *Him*. His Lord Himself has *bid* him look for Him in the signs of the

[1] 1 Cor. vi. 12.

world, and therefore he looks out. His Lord Himself has shown him, in the Old Testament, how He, the Lord of Glory, condescends to humble Himself to the things of heaven and earth. He knows that God's Angels are about the earth. He knows that once they were even used to come in human shape. He knows that the Son of God, ere now, has come on earth. He knows that He promised to His Church the presence of a miraculous agency, and has never recalled His promise. Again, he reads, in the Book of the Revelation, quite enough, not to show him what is coming, but to show him that now, as heretofore, a secret supernatural system is going on *under* this visible scene. And therefore he looks out for Christ, for His present providences, and for His coming; and, though often deceived in his expectation, and fancying wonderful things are coming on the earth, when they still delay, he uses, and comforts him with the Prophet's words,

> I will stand upon my watch, and set me upon the tower, and will watch to see what He will say unto me, and what I shall answer when I am reproved. And the Lord answered me. . . . The vision is yet for an appointed time, but at the end it shall speak and not lie; though it tarry, wait for it, because it will surely come, it will not tarry. Behold, his soul, which is lifted up, is not upright in him; but the just shall live by his faith.[1]*

[1] Hab. ii. 1–4.

*'Waiting for Christ', *PPS*, VI, Sermon 17.

---

## SUBJECTION OF THE REASON
## AND FEELINGS TO THE
## REVEALED WORD
### (ASCENSION)

*2 COR. X. 5*
'*Bringing into captivity every thought to the obedience of Christ.*'

THE question may be asked, How is it possible to live as if the coming of Christ were not far off, when our reason tells us that it probably is distant? It may be objected that there are no grounds for expecting it now, more than for the last eighteen hundred years; that if His long absence is a reason for expecting it now, yet His promise of a speedy return was a reason for expecting it in earlier times; and if the one reason has turned out insufficient, so may the other; that if, in spite of His promise to be speedy, He has tarried so long, He may tarry longer still; that no signs of His coming can be greater than were abroad soon after His departure; that, certainly, there are no such signs now; nay, that during the first seven hundred years, and again about the year 1000, and later, there were many more signs of Christ's coming than there are now—more trouble of nations, more distress, more sickness, more terror. It may be said that we cannot hope, and fear, and expect, and wait, as we will— but that we must have *reasons* for so doing; and that if we are persuaded, in our deliberate judgment, that Christ's coming is not probable, we cannot make ourselves feel as if it were probable.

Now in considering this objection, which I shall do, I may have an opportunity of stating a great principle which obtains in Christian duty, the subjection of the whole mind to the law of God.

1. I deny, then, that our feelings and likings are only moved according to the dictates of what we commonly mean by reason; so far from it, that nothing is more common, on the other hand, than to say that reason goes one way, and our wishes go another. There is nothing impossible, then, in learning to look out for the day of Christ's coming more earnestly than according to its probability in the judgment of reason. As reason may be a right guide for our feelings and likings to go by up to a certain point, so there may be cases in which it is unable to guide us, from its weakness; and as it is not impossible for sinful and irreligious men to like what their reason tells them they should not like; therefore it is not impossible for religious men also to desire, expect, and hope, what their reason is unequal to approve and accept. What is more common than to hear it said, 'I love a person more than I respect him'? or, 'I admire him more than I love him'? Or, again, we know how easy it is to open the mind to the influence of some feeling or emotion, and how difficult it is to avoid such influence; how difficult it is to get a thought out of the mind, which reason says ought to be kept out, and which will intrude itself again and again; how difficult to restrain anger, fear, or other passion, which yet reason tells us should be restrained. It is, then, quite possible to have feelings and thoughts present with us in a way which is disproportionate, according to the judgment of reason. Or, take another instance. We know how the mind sometimes

dwells upon the chance of what is barely possible, quite un-reasonably, and often wrongly and dangerously. A number of things may happen, one perhaps as likely as another; and yet, from weakness of health, or excitement, it often happens that we cannot help thinking overmuch of some one of these possible events, and getting unduly anxious lest it should happen. Thus, if some dreadful occurrence has taken place, a fire, or a murder, or some horrible accident, persons become frightened, lest the same should happen to them, in a measure far exceeding what a mere calculation of probabilities warrants. Their imagination magnifies the danger; they cannot persuade themselves to look at things calmly, and according to their general course. They fix their thoughts upon one particular chance, in a way quite contrary to what reason suggests. Thus, so far from our feelings being moved according to the strict probabilities of things, the contrary is rather the rule. What Almighty God then requires of us is, to do that in one instance for His sake, which we do so commonly in indulgence of our own way-wardness and weakness; to hope, fear, expect our Lord's coming, more than reason warrants, and in a way which His word alone warrants; that is, to trust Him above our reason. You say, that it is not probable Christ will come at this time, and therefore you cannot expect it. Now, I say, you can expect it. You must feel there is a chance that He will come. Well, then, dwell on that chance; open your mind to it; treat that chance just as you so often treat the chance of fire, or peril by sea, or peril by land, or thieves. Our Lord says, that He shall come as a thief in the night. Now you know that if there has been some remarkable robbery, people are frightened far more than according to the chance of their being themselves robbed. They are haunted by the idea; it may be that the probability of their

own houses being attempted is but small, yet the thing itself
is an object of great apprehension to them, and they think
more of the grievousness of the event apprehended, should
it happen, than of the small chance of its happening. They
are moved by the risk. And in like manner, as regards the
coming of Christ; I do not say we must be excited, or unsettled, or engrossed with the thought, but still we must
not let the long delay persuade us not to watch for it.
'Though it tarry, wait for it.' If He bids us, as a matter of
duty, impress the prospect of His coming upon our imagination, He asks no hard thing; no hard thing, that is, to the
willing mind; and what we can do we are bound to do.

2. This is what first suggests itself, but it opens the way
to further thoughts. For only reflect, what is faith itself but
an acceptance of things unseen, from the love of them,
*beyond* the determinations of calculation and experience?
Faith outstrips argument. If there is only a fair chance that
the Bible is true, that heaven is the reward of obedience,
and hell of wilful sin, it is worth while, it is safe, to sacrifice
this world to the next. It were worth while, though Christ
told us to sell all that we have and follow Him, and to pass
our time here in poverty and contempt, it were worth while
on that chance to do it. This, then, is what is meant by faith
going against reason, that it cares not for the measure of
probabilities; it does not ask whether a thing is more or less
likely; but if there is a fair and clear likelihood what God's
will is, it acts upon it. If Scripture were not true, we should
in the next world be left where we were; we should, in the
event, be no worse off than before; but if it be true, then
we shall be infinitely worse off for not believing it than if
we had believed it. We all know the retort which the aged
saint made in the story, when a licentious youth reminded
him, how he would have wasted life if there were *no* future

state of recompense: 'True, my son,' he answered, 'but how *much* worse a waste is yours if there *is*.'

Faith, then, does not regard *degrees* of evidence. You might lay it down as a rule, speaking in the way of reason, that we ought to have faith according to the evidence; that the more evidence there is, the more firm it should be; and the less evidence, the weaker will it be required of us. But this is not the case as regards religious faith—which accepts the Word of God as firmly on the evidence which it is vouchsafed, as if that evidence were doubled. This, indeed, we see to be the case as regards things of earth; and surely what we do towards men, we may bear to do towards God. If anyone whom we trust and revere told us any news, which he had perfect means of knowing, we should believe him; we should not believe it more thoroughly because presently another told it to us also. And in like manner, though it is quite certain that Almighty God might have given us greater evidence than we possess, that He speaks to us in the Bible; yet since He has given us enough, faith does not ask for more, but is satisfied, and acts upon what *is* enough; whereas unbelief is ever asking for signs, more and greater, before it will yield to the Divine Word.

Returning to my main subject, I observe, in like manner, what is true of faith is true of hope. We may be commanded, if so be, to hope against hope, or to expect Christ's coming, in a certain sense, against reason. It is not inconsistent with God's general dealings towards us that He should bid us feel and act as if that were at hand which yet, if we went by what experience tells us, we should say was not likely to be at hand. If He bids us to believe in Him with our whole heart, whether the evidence of His speaking to us be greater or less, why may He not bid us wait for Him perseveringly, though the signs of His coming disappoint us, and reason desponds? We cannot tell in such a matter what is more probable and what is not; we can but attempt what we are told to do. And *that* we can do: we can direct and fashion our feelings according to His word, and leave the rest to Him.

3. Here, then, I am led to make a further remark; that as it is our duty to bring some things before our minds, and contemplate them much more vividly than reason by itself would bid us, so, again, there are other things which it is a duty to put away from us, not to dwell upon, and not to realize, though they be brought before us. And yet it is evident, too, that persons might here also object, and say that it is impossible to help being moved and influenced by what we know for certain, just as they say that it is impossible to believe and expect what we know to be not certain.

For instance; we know that it is a duty not to be vain and conceited about any personal advantage we may happen to possess. Yet a man might ask, How is it possible to help it? He might say,

> If persons excel in any respect, they must know it; it is quite absurd to suppose, as a rule, that they should not; but if they know it, how is it possible they should not take pleasure in their own excellence, and admire themselves for it? Admiration is the natural consequence of the sight of excellence: if persons know they excel, they cannot help admiring themselves; and if they excel, generally speaking, they cannot but know it; and this, whatever it be they excel in, whether in personal appearance, or in power of speech, or in gifts of mind, or in character, or in any other way.

But now, on the other hand, I suppose that it is quite certain that Scripture tells us *not* to pride ourselves on any-thing we are, anything we do; that is, not to indulge those feelings which, it seems, are the natural and legitimate result of our knowing what we do know. Now what is to be said to this? How are these opposites to be reconciled?

One answer would of course be this; that religious men know how defective, after all, their best deeds are, or their best points of character; or they know how much more others do; or they know their own great deficiencies in other respects; or they know how trifling some of those points are on which they may happen to be superior to others. But this is not a sufficient answer; because the points in question *are* excellences, whether great excellences or not, or whether or not there be others greater, or however wanting the parties may be in other respects. And herein lies, I think, the temptation which all persons have to self-esteem, that in a certain sense their judgment about themselves is not wrong; not that they are not very deficient in many things, not as if they did not know this, but that they *have* certain excellences, which really *are* excellences, and they *feel* them; and the question is, how can they help feeling them?

It may be suggested, perhaps, to account for the humility of religious men, that, whatever personal gifts they may have, they are *used* to them; and this it is which keeps them from thinking much of them. There is truth in this remark, of course, but it does not explain why they *once* have not thought much of them, viz. when the sight of what they were, was not so familiar to them as it is; and if they did, we may be sure that the effects of their former self-conceit will remain upon them now, having become habitual.

Another and far better reason why religious persons are not self-conceited is that they dislike to think of whatever is good in them, and turn away from the thought of it, whether their superiority to others be in mind or body, in intellectual powers or in moral attainments. But there is, I think, another more direct reason, and more connected with my present subject.

It is this: though religious men have gifts, and though they know it, yet they do not *realize* them. It is not necessary here to explain exactly what is meant by the word 'realizing'; we all understand the word enough for my present purpose, and shall all confess that, at least, there is an abundance of matters which men do *not* realize, though they ought to do so. For instance; how loudly men talk of the shortness of this life, of its vanity and unprofitableness, and of the claims which the world to come has upon us! This is what we hear said daily, yet few act upon the truths they utter; and why? Because they do not *realize* what they are so ready to proclaim. They do not see Him who is invisible, and His external kingdom.

Well, then, what men omit to do when the doing is a duty, that they can surely also omit to do in cases when omission is a duty. Serious men may know indeed, if it so be, what their excellences are, whether religious, or moral, or any other, but they do not feel them in that vivid way which we call realizing. They do not open their hearts to the knowledge, so that it becomes fruitful. Barren knowledge is a wretched thing, when knowledge ought to bear fruit; but it is a good thing, when it would otherwise act merely as a temptation. When men realize a truth, it becomes an influential principle within them, and leads to a number of consequences both in opinion and in conduct. The case is the same as regards realizing our own gifts. But men of superior minds know them without realizing. They may know that they have certain excellences, if they have them, they may know that they have good points of character, or abilities, or attainments; but it is in the way of an unproductive knowledge, which leaves the mind just as it found it. And this seems to be what gives such a remarkable simplicity to the character of holy men, and amazes others so much that they think it a pradadox or inconsistency, or even a mark of insincerity, that the same persons should profess to know so much about themselves, and yet so little —that they can hear so much said about themselves, that they can bear so much praise, so much popularity, so much deference, and yet without being puffed up, or arrogating aught, or despising others; that they can speak about themselves, yet in so unaffected a tone, with so much nature, with such childlike innocence, and such graceful frankness.

Another instance of this great gift of knowing without realizing, is afforded us in relation to subjects to which I will but allude. Men who indulge their passions have a knowledge, different in kind from those who have abstained from such indulgence; and when they speak on subjects connected with it, realize them in a way in which others cannot realize them. The very ideas which are full of temptation to the former, the words which are painful to them to utter, all that causes them shame and confusion of face, can be said and thought of by the innocent without any distress at all. Angels can look upon sin with simple abhorrence and wonder, without humiliation or secret emotion; and a like simplicity is the reward of the chaste and holy; and that to the great amazement of the unclean, who cannot understand the state of mind of such a one, or how he can utter or endure thoughts which to themselves are full of misery and guilt. And hence sometimes you find men in these days, in which the will of the natural man is indulged to the full, taking up the writings of holy men who have lived in deserts or in cloisters, or with an Angel's heart have ruled Christ's flock, and broken with holy hands the bread of life, and viewing their words in their own murky atmosphere, and imputing to them their own grossness; nay, carping at the words of Holy Scripture, which are God's, and at the words of the Church, as if the sacred mystery of the Incarnation had not introduced a thousand new and heavenly associations into this world of sin.

And hence, again, you will find self-indulgent men unable to comprehend the real existence of sanctity and severity of mind in anyone. They think that all persons must be full of the same wretched thoughts and feelings which torment themselves. They think that none can avoid it, from the nature of the case; only that certain persons contrive to hide what goes on in their hearts, and, in consequence, they call them pretenders and hypocrites.

This, too, is what they also say as regards the instance which I took first—a man's knowledge of his gifts. They think that men who appear to think little of themselves are conceited within, and that what is called modesty is affectation.

I might make the same remark also as regards the absence of resentment upon injury or insult, which characterizes a really religious man. Often, indeed, such a one feels keenly what is done against him, though he represses the feeling as a matter of duty; but the higher state of mind is when he does not feel, that is, when he does not realize, that any injustice has been done him; so that if he attempts to speak of it, it will be in the same sort of strange, unreal, and (as I may say) forced and unnatural way in which pretenders to religion speak of religious joy and spiritual comfort, for he is as little at home with anger and revenge as hypocrites are with thoughts of heaven.

Again; we may so unduly realize that a life of virtue is for our interest, as to act on prudential motives, not from a sense of duty. And again; though it be our duty to inquire and search out for ourselves the truth in religious matters, yet we may so vaunt in our private judgment, and make a merit of the exercise of it, that our search becomes almost a sin.

Here then are a number of cases, all in point, to illustrate one and the same truth, that the Christian's character is formed by a rule higher than that of calculation and reason, consisting in a Divine principle or life, which transcends the anticipations and criticisms of ordinary men. Judging by mere worldly reason, the Christian ought to be self-conceited, for he is gifted; he ought to understand evil, because he sees and speaks of it; he ought to feel resentment, because he is conscious of being injured; he ought to act from self-interest, because he knows that what is right is also expedient; he ought to be conscious and fond of the exercises of private judgment, because he engages in them; he ought to be doubting and hesitating in his faith, because his evidence for it might be greater than it is; he ought to have no expectation of Christ's coming, because Christ has delayed so long; but not so: his mind and heart are formed on a different mould. In these, and ten thousand other ways, he is open to the misapprehensions of the world, which neither has his feelings nor can enter into them. Nor can he explain and defend them on considerations which all men, good and bad, can understand. He goes by a law which others know not; not his own wisdom or judgment, but by Christ's wisdom and the judgment of the Spirit, which is imparted to him—by that inward incommunicable perception of truth and duty which is the rule of his reason, affections, wishes, tastes, and all that is in him, and which is the result of persevering obedience. This it is which gives so unearthly a character to his whole life and conversation, which is 'hid with Christ in God'; he has ascended with Christ on high, and there 'in heart and mind continually dwells'; and he is obliged, in consequence, to put a veil upon his face, and is mysterious in the world's judgment, and 'becomes as it were a monster unto many', though he be 'wiser than the aged', and have 'more understanding than his teachers, because he keeps God's commandments'. Thus 'he that is spiritual judgeth all things, yet he himself is judged of no man'; and with him 'it is a very small thing to be judged of man's judgment', for 'He that judgeth him is the Lord'.[1]

One additional remark is necessary in conclusion, with reference to the subject with which I began, the duty of waiting for our Lord's coming. It must not be supposed, then, that this implies a neglect of our duties in this world. As it is possible to watch for Christ in spite of earthly reasonings to the contrary, so is it possible to engage in earthly duties, in spite of our watching. Christ has told us that when He comes two men shall be in the field, two women at the mill, 'the one shall be taken, and the other left.' You see that good and bad are engaged in the same way; nor need it hinder anyone from having his heart firmly fixed on God, that he is engaged in worldly business with those whose hearts are upon the world. Nay, we may form large plans, we may busy ourselves in new undertakings, we may begin great works which we cannot do more than begin; we may make provision for the future, and anticipate in our acts the certainty of centuries to come, yet be looking out for Christ. Thus indeed we are bound to proceed, and to leave 'times and seasons in His Father's power.' Whenever He comes, He will cut things short; and, for what we know, our efforts and beginnings, though they be nothing more, are just as necessary in the

---

[1] 1 Cor. ii. 15; iv. 3, 4.

course of His Providence as could be the most successful accomplishment. Surely, He will end the world abruptly, whenever He comes; He will break off the designs and labours of His elect, whatever they are, and give them what their dutiful anxiety aims at, though not through it. And, as He will end, so did He begin the world abruptly; He began the world which we see, not from its first seeds and elements, but He created at once the herb and the fruit-tree perfect 'whose seed is in itself', not a gradual formation, but a complete work. And with even a greater abruptness did He display His miracles when He came and new made all things, creating bread, not corn, for the supply of the five thousand, and changing water, not into any simpler, though precious liquid, but into wine. And as He began without beginning, so will He end without an ending; or rather, all that we do—whatever we are doing—whether we have time for more or time for less—yet our work, finished or unfinished, will be acceptable, if done for Him. There is no inconsistency, then, in watching yet working, for we may work without setting our hearts on our work. Our sin will be if we idolize the work of our hands; if we love it so well as not to bear to part with it. The test of our faith lies in our being able to fail without disappointment.

Let us pray God to rule our hearts in this respect as well as in others; that 'when He shall appear, we may have confidence, and not be ashamed before Him at His coming.'*

*'The Subjection of the Reason and Feelings to the Revealed Word', *PPS*, VI, Sermon 18.

# 12. THE CHRISTIAN CHARACTER

## EQUANIMITY
### (CHRISTMAS)

*PHIL. IV. 4*
*'Rejoice in the Lord alway, and again I say, Rejoice.'*

IN other parts of Scripture the prospect of Christ's coming is made a reason for solemn fear and awe, and a call
for watching and prayer, but in the verses connected with
the text a distinct view of the Christian character is set
before us, and distinct duties urged on us. 'The Lord is at
hand,' and what then?—why, if so, we must 'rejoice in the
Lord'; we must be conspicuous for 'moderation'; we must
be 'careful for nothing'; we must seek from God's bounty,
and not from man, whatever we need; we must abound in
'thanksgiving'; and we must cherish, or rather we must
pray for, and we shall receive from above, 'the peace of God
which passeth all understanding', to 'keep our hearts and
minds through Christ Jesus'.

Now this is a view of the Christian character definite and
complete enough to admit of commenting on—and it may
be useful to show that the thought of Christ's coming not
only leads to fear, but to a calm and cheerful frame of
mind.

Nothing perhaps is more remarkable than that an
Apostle—a man of toil and blood, a man combating with
powers unseen, and a spectacle for men and Angels, and

much more that St. Paul, a man whose natural temper was so zealous, so severe, and so vehement—I say, nothing is more striking and significant than that St. Paul should have given us this view of what a Christian should be. It would be nothing wonderful, it *is* nothing wonderful, that writers in a day like this should speak of peace, quiet, sobriety, and cheerfulness, as being the tone of mind that becomes a Christian; but considering that St. Paul was by birth a Jew, and by education a Pharisee, that he wrote at a time when, if at any time, Christians were in lively and incessant agitation of mind; when persecution and rumours of persecution abounded; when all things seemed in commotion around them; when there was nothing fixed; when there were no churches to soothe them, no course of worship to sober them, no homes to refresh them; and, again, considering that the Gospel is full of high and noble, and what may be called even romantic, principles and motives, and deep mysteries —and, further, considering the very topic which the Apostle combines with his admonitions is that awful subject, the coming of Christ—it is well worthy of notice that, in such a time, under such a covenant, and with such a prospect, he should draw a picture of the Christian character as free from excitement and effort, as full of repose, as still and as equable, as if the great Apostle wrote in some monastery of the desert or some country parsonage. Here surely is the finger of God; here is the evidence of supernatural influences, making the mind of man independent of circumstances! This is the thought that first suggests itself; and the second is this, how deep and refined is the true Christian spirit!—how difficult to enter into, how vast to embrace, how impossible to exhaust! Who would expect such composure and equanimity from the fervent Apostle of the Gentiles? We know St. Paul could do great things; could

suffer and achieve, could preach and confess, could be high
and could be low: but we might have thought that all this
was the limit and the perfection of the Christian temper, as
he viewed it; and that no room was left him for the feelings
which the text and following verses lead us to ascribe to
him.

And yet he who 'laboured more abundantly than all' his
brethren is also a pattern of simplicity, meekness, cheerfulness, thankfulness, and serenity of mind. These tempers
were especially characteristic of St. Paul, and are much
insisted on in his Epistles. For instance—'Mind not high
things, but condescend to men of low estate. Be not wise in
your own conceits. . . . Provide things honest in the sight of
all men. If it be possible, as much as lieth in you, live
peaceably with all men.' He enjoins, that 'the aged men be
sober, grave, temperate, sound in faith, in charity, in
patience'. 'The aged woman likewise . . . not false accusers,
not given to much wine, teachers of good things, that they
may teach the young women to be sober, to love their
husbands, to love their children, to be discreet, chaste,
keepers at home, good, obedient to their own husbands.'
And 'young men' to be 'sober-minded'. And it is remarkable that he ends this exhortation with urging the same
reason as is given in the verse after the text: 'looking for
that blessed hope, and the glorious appearing of our great
God and Saviour Jesus Christ'. In like manner, he says, that
Christ's ministers must show 'uncorruptness in doctrine,
gravity, sincerity, sound speech that cannot be condemned'; that they must be 'blameless, not self-willed, not
soon angry . . . lovers of good men, sober, just, holy, temperate'.[1] All this is the description of what seems almost an
ordinary character; I mean, it is so staid, so quiet, so

[1] Rom. xii. 16–18; Titus ii. 2–13; i. 7, 8.

unambitious, so homely. It displays so little of what is striking or extraordinary. It is so negligent of this world, so
unexcited, so singleminded.

It is observable, too, that it was foretold as the peculiar-
ity of Gospel times by the Prophet Isaiah: 'The work of
righteousness shall be peace; and the effect of righteousness,
quietness and assurance for ever. And My people shall dwell
in a peaceable habitation, and in sure dwellings, and in
quiet resting-places.'[1]

Now then let us consider more particularly what is this
state of mind, and what the grounds of it. These seem to be
as follows: The Lord is at hand; this is not your rest; this
is not your abiding-place. Act then as persons who are in
a dwelling not their own; who are not in their own home;
who have not their own goods and furniture about them;
who, accordingly, make shift and put up with anything that
comes to hand, and do not make a point of things being the
best of their kind. 'But this I say, brethren, the time is
short.' What matters it what we eat, what we drink, how
we are clothed, where we lodge, what is thought of us, what
becomes of us, since we are not at home? It is felt every day,
even as regards this world, that when we leave home for a
while we are unsettled. This, then, is the kind of feeling
which a belief in Christ's coming will create within us. It
is not worth while establishing ourselves here; it is not
worth while spending time and thought on such an object.
We shall hardly have got settled when we shall have to
move.

This being apparently the general drift of the passage,
let us next enter into the particular portions of it.

1. 'Be careful for nothing,' he says, or, as St. Peter,
'casting all your care upon Him', or, as He Himself, 'Take

[1] Isa. xxxii. 17, 18.

no thought' or care 'for the morrow, for the morrow will take thought for the things of itself'.[1] This of course is the state of mind which is directly consequent on the belief, that 'the Lord is at hand'. Who would care for any loss or gain today, if he knew for certain that Christ would show Himself tomorrow? No one. Well, then, the true Christian feels as he would feel, did he know for certain that Christ would be here tomorrow. For he knows for certain that at least Christ will come to him when he dies; and faith anticipates his death, and makes it just as if that distant day, if it *be* distant, were past and over. One time or another Christ will come, for certain: and when He once *has* come, it matters not what length of time there was before He came; however long that period may be, it has an end. Judgment is coming, whether it comes sooner or later, and the Christian realizes that it is coming; that is, time does not enter into his calculation, or interfere with his view of things. When men expect to carry out their plans and projects, then they care for them; when they know these will come to nought, they give them over, or become indifferent to them.

So, again, it is with all forebodings, anxieties, mortifications, griefs, resentments of this world. 'The time is short.' It has sometimes been well suggested, as a mode of calming the mind when set upon an object, or much vexed or angered at some occurrence, what will you feel about all this a year hence? It is very plain that matters which agitate us most extremely now will then interest us not at all; that objects about which we have intense hope and fear now, will then be to us nothing more than things which happen at the other end of the earth. So will it be with all human hopes, fears, pleasures, pains, jealousies, disappointments,

[1] 1 Peter v. 7; Matt. vi. 34.

successes, when the last day is come. They will have no life in them; they will be as the faded flowers of a banquet, which do but mock us. Or when we lie on the bed of death, what will it avail is to have been rich, or great, or fortunate, or honoured, or influential? All things will then be vanity. Well, what this world will be understood by all to be then, such is it felt to be by the Christian now. He looks at things as he then will look at them, with an uninterested and dispassionate eye, and is neither pained much nor pleased much at the accidents of life, because they are accidents.

2. Another part of the character under review is, what our translation calls moderation; 'Let your moderation be known unto all men', or, as it may be more exactly rendered, your consideration, fairness, or equitableness. St. Paul makes it a part of a Christian character to have a reputation for candour, dispassionateness, tenderness towards others. The truth is, as soon and in proportion as a person believes that Christ is coming, and recognizes his own position as a stranger on earth, who has but hired a lodging in it for a season, he will feel indifferent to the course of human affairs. He will be able to look on, instead of taking a part in them. They will be nothing to him. He will be able to criticize them, and pass judgment on them, without partiality. This is what is meant by 'our moderation' being acknowledged by all men. Those who have strong interests one way or the other, cannot be dispassionate observers and candid judges. They are partisans; they defend one set of people and attack another. They are prejudiced against those who differ from them, or who thwart them. They cannot make allowances, or show sympathy for them. But the Christian has no keen expectations, no acute mortifications. He is fair, equitable, considerate towards all men, because he has no temptation to be otherwise. He

has no violence, no animosity, no bigotry, no party feeling. He knows that his Lord and Saviour must triumph; he knows that He will one day come from heaven, no one can say how soon. Knowing then the end to which all things tend, he cares less for the road which is to lead to it. When we read a book of fiction, we are much excited with the course of the narrative, till we know how things will turn out; but when we do, the interest ceases. So is it with the Christian. He knows Christ's battle will last till the end; that Christ's cause will triumph in the end; that His Church will last till He comes. He knows what is truth and what is error, where is safety and where is danger; and all this clear knowledge enables him to make concessions, to own difficulties, to do justice to the erring, to acknowledge their good points, to be content with such countenance, greater or less, as he himself receives from others. He does not fear; fear it is that makes men bigots, tyrants, and zealots; but for the Christian, it is his privilege, as he is beyond hopes and fears, suspense and jealousy, so also to be patient, cool, discriminating, and impartial; so much so that this very fairness marks his character in the eyes of the world, is 'known unto all men'.

3. Joy and gladness are also characteristics of him, according to the exhortation in the text, 'Rejoice in the Lord alway', and this in spite of the fear and awe which the thought of the Last Day ought to produce in him. It is by means of these strong contrasts that Scripture brings out to us what is the real meaning of its separate portions. If we had been told merely to fear, we should have mistaken a slavish dread, or the gloom of despair, for godly fear; and if we had been told merely to rejoice, we should perhaps have mistaken a rude freedom and familiarity for joy; but when we are told both to fear and to rejoice, we gain thus

much at first sight, that our joy is not to be irreverent, nor our fear to be desponding; that though both feelings are to remain, neither is to be what it would be by itself. This is what we gain at once by such contrasts. I do not say that this makes it at all easier to combine the separate duties to which they relate; that is a further and higher work; but thus much we gain at once, a better knowledge of those separate duties themselves. And now I am speaking about the duty of rejoicing, and I say that whatever be the duty of fearing greatly and trembling greatly at the thought of the Day of Judgment, and of course it is a great duty, yet the command so to do cannot reverse the command to rejoice; it can only so far interfere with it as to explain what is meant by rejoicing. It is as clear a duty to rejoice in the prospect of Christ's coming as if we were not told to fear it. The duty of fearing does but perfect our joy; that joy alone is true Christian joy, which is informed and quickened by fear, and made thereby sober and reverent.

How joy and fear can be reconciled, words cannot show. Act and deed alone can show how. Let a man try both to fear and to rejoice, as Christ and His Apostles tell him, and in time he will learn how; but when he has learned, he will be as little able to explain how it is he does both, as he was before. He will seem inconsistent, and may easily be proved to be so, to the satisfaction of irreligious men as Scripture is called inconsistent. He becomes the paradox which Scripture enjoins. This is variously fulfilled in the case of men of advanced holiness. They are accused of the most opposite faults; of being proud, and of being mean; of being over-simple, and being crafty; of having too strict, and, at the same time, too lax a conscience; of being un-social, and yet being worldly; of being too literal in ex-plaining Scripture, and yet of adding to Scripture, and superseding Scripture. Men of the world, or men of inferior religiousness, cannot understand them, and are fond of criticizing those who, in seeming to be inconsistent, are but like Scripture teaching.

But to return to the case of joy and fear. It may be objected that at least those who fall into sin, or who have in times past sinned grievously, cannot have this pleasant and cheerful temper which St. Paul enjoins. I grant it. But what is this but saying that St. Paul enjoins us *not* to fall into sin? When St. Paul warns us against sadness and heaviness, of course he warns us against those things which make men sad and heavy; and therefore especially against sin, which is an especial enemy of joyfulness. It is not that sorrowing for sin is wrong when we *have* sinned, but the *sinning* is wrong which causes the sorrowing. When a person has sinned, he cannot do anything better than sorrow. He ought to sorrow; and so far as he does sorrow, he is certainly *not* in the perfect Christian state; but it is his sin that has forfeited it. And yet even here sorrow is not inconsistent with rejoicing. For there are few men, who are really in earnest in their sorrow, but after a time may be conscious that they are so; and, when man knows himself to be in earnest, he knows that God looks mercifully upon him; and this gives him sufficient reason for rejoicing, even though fear remains. St. Peter could appeal to Christ, 'Lord, Thou knowest all things; Thou knowest that I love Thee.' We of course cannot appeal so unreservedly—still we can timidly appeal—we can say that we humbly trust that, whatever be the measure of our past sins, and whatever of our present self-denial, yet at bottom we do wish and strive to give up the world and to follow Christ; and in proportion as this sense of sincerity is strong upon our minds, in the same degree shall we rejoice in the Lord, even while we fear.

4. Once more, peace is part of this same temper also. 'The peace of God,' says the Apostle, 'which passeth all understanding, shall keep your hearts and minds through Christ Jesus.' There are many things in the Gospel to alarm us, many to agitate us, many to transport us, but the end and issue of all these is *peace*. 'Glory to God in the highest, and on earth peace.' It may be asked indeed whether warfare, perplexity, and uncertainty be not the condition of the Christian here below; whether St. Paul himself does not say that he has 'the care', or the anxiety, 'of all the Churches', and whether he does not plainly evince and avow in his Epistles to the Galatians and Corinthians much distress of mind? 'Without were fightings, within fears'.[1] I grant it; he certainly shows at times much agitation of mind; but consider this. Did you ever look at an expanse of water, and observe the ripples on the surface? Do you think that disturbance penetrates below it? Nay; you have seen or heard of fearful tempests on the sea; scenes of horror and distress, which are in no respect a fit type of an Apostle's tears or sighings about his flock. Yet even these violent commotions do not reach into the depths. The foundations of the ocean, the vast realms of water which girdle the earth, are as tranquil and as silent in the storm as in a calm. So is it with the souls of holy men. They have a well of peace springing up within them unfathomable; and though the accidents of the hour may make them seem agitated, yet in their hearts they are not so. Even Angels joy over sinners repentant, and, as we may therefore suppose, grieve over sinners impenitent—yet who shall say that they have not perfect peace? Even Almighty God Himself deigns to speak of His being grieved, and angry, and rejoicing—yet is He not the unchangeable? And in like manner, to compare human

[1] 2 Cor. vii. 5.

things with divine, St. Paul had perfect peace, as being stayed in soul on God, though the trials of life might vex him.

For, as I have said, the Christian has a deep, silent, hidden peace, which the world sees not—like some well in a retired and shady place, difficult of access. He is the greater part of his time by himself, and when he is in solitude, that is his real state. What he is when left to himself and to his God, that is his true life. He can bear himself; he can (as it were) joy in himself, for it is the grace of God within him, it is the presence of the Eternal Comforter, in which he joys. He can bear, he finds it pleasant, to be with himself at all times—'never less alone than when alone'. He can lay his head on his pillow at night, and own in God's sight, with overflowing heart, that he wants nothing—that he 'is full and abounds'—that God has been all things to him, and that nothing is not his which God could give him. More thankfulness, more holiness, more of heaven he needs indeed, but the thought that he can have more is not a thought of trouble, but of joy. It does not interfere with his peace to know that he may grow nearer God. Such is the Christian's peace, when, with a single heart and the Cross in his eye, he addresses and commends himself to Him with whom the night is as clear as the day. St. Paul says that 'the peace of God shall *keep* our hearts and minds'. By 'keep' is meant 'guard', or 'garrison', our hearts; so as to keep out enemies. And he says, our 'hearts and minds' in contrast to what the world sees of us. Many hard things may be said of the Christian, and done against him, but he has a secret preservative or charm, and minds them not.

These are some few suggestions on that character of mind which becomes the followers of Him who was once 'born of a pure Virgin', and who bids them as 'new-born

babes desire the sincere milk of the Word, that they may
grow thereby'. The Christian is cheerful, easy, kind, gentle,
courteous, candid, unassuming; has no pretence, no affectation, no ambition, no singularity; because he has neither
hope nor fear about this world. He is serious, sober, discreet,
grave, moderate, mild, with so little that is unusual or striking in his bearing that he may easily be taken at first sight
for an ordinary man. There are persons who think religion
consists in ecstasies, or in set speeches; he is not of those.
And it must be confessed, on the other hand, that there is a
commonplace state of mind which does show itself calm,
composed, and candid, yet is very far from the true Christian
temper. In this day especially it is very easy for men to be
benevolent, liberal, and dispassionate. It costs nothing to
be dispassionate when you feel nothing, to be cheerful when
you have nothing to fear, to be generous or liberal when
what you give is not your own, and to be benevolent and
considerate when you have no principles and no opinions.
Men nowadays are moderate and equitable, not because
the Lord is at hand, but because they do not feel that He is
coming. Quietness is a grace, not in itself, only when it is graft-
ed on the stem of faith, zeal, self-abasement, and diligence.

May it be our blessedness, as years go on, to add one
grace to another, and advance upward, step by step, neither
neglecting the lower after attaining the higher, nor aiming
at the higher before attaining the lower. The first grace is
faith, the last is love; first comes zeal, afterwards comes
loving-kindness; first comes humiliation, then comes peace;
first comes diligence, then comes resignation. May we learn
to mature all graces in us; fearing and trembling, watching
and repenting, because Christ is coming; joyful, thankful,
and careless of the future, because He is come.*

*'Equanimity', *PPS*, V, Sermon 5.

## PEACE IN BELIEVING
### (TRINITY SUNDAY)

*ISAIAH VI. 3*
'*And one cried unto another, and said, Holy, Holy, Holy, is the Lord of Hosts.*'

EVERY Lord's day is a day of rest, but this, perhaps, more than any. It commemorates, not an act of God, however gracious and glorious, but His own unspeakable perfections and adorable mysteriousness. It is a day especially sacred to peace. Our Lord left His peace with us when He went away; 'Peace I leave with you; My peace I give unto you: not as the world giveth, give I unto you';[1] and He said He would send them a Comforter, who should give them peace. Last week we commemorated that Comforter's coming; and today we commemorate in an especial way the gift He brought with Him, in that great doctrine which is its emblem and its means. 'These things have I spoken unto you, that in Me ye might have peace: in the world ye shall have tribulation.'[2] Christ here says, that instead of this world's troubles, He gives His disciples peace; and, accordingly, in today's Collect, we pray that we may be kept in the faith of the Eternal Trinity in Unity, *and* be 'defended from all adversities', for in keeping that faith we are kept from trouble.

[1] John xiv. 27.
[2] John xvi. 33.

Hence, too, in the blessing which Moses told the priests to pronounce over the children of Israel, God's Name is put upon them, and that three times, in order to bless and keep them, to make His face shine on them, and to give them peace. And hence again, in our own solemn form of blessing, with which we end our public service, we impart to the people 'the peace of God, which passeth all understanding', and 'the blessing of the Father, the Son, and the Holy Ghost'.

God is the God of peace, and in giving us peace He does but give Himself, He does but manifest Himself to us; for His presence is peace. Hence our Lord, in the same discourse in which He promised His disciples peace, promised also that 'He would come and manifest Himself unto them', that 'He and His Father would come to them, and make Their abode with them'.[1] Peace is His everlasting state; in this world of space and time He has wrought and acted; but from everlasting it was not so. For six days He wrought, and then He rested according to that rest which was His eternal state; yet not so rested, as not in one sense to 'work hitherto', in mercy and in judgment, towards that world which He had created. And more especially, when He sent His Only-begotten Son into the world, and that most Gracious and All-pitiful Son, our Lord, condescended to come to us, both He and His Father wrought with a mighty hand; and They vouchsafed the Holy Ghost, the Comforter, and He also wrought wonderfully, and works hitherto. Certainly the whole economy of redemption is a series of great and continued works; but still they all tend to rest and peace, as at the first. They began out of rest, and they end in rest. They end in that eternal state out of which they began. The Son was from eternity in the bosom of the Father, as His dearly-

[1] John xiv. 21, 23.

beloved and Only-begotten. He loved Him before the foundation of the world. He had glory with Him before the world was. He was in the Father, and the Father in Him. None knew the Son but the Father, nor the Father but the Son. 'In the beginning was the Word, and the Word was with God, and the Word was God.' He was 'the Brightness of God's glory and the express Image of His Person'; and in this unspeakable Unity of Father and Son, was the Spirit also, as being the Spirit of the Father, and the Spirit of the Son; the Spirit of Both at once, not separate from them, yet distinct, so that they were Three Persons, One God, from everlasting.

Thus was it, we are told, from everlasting; before the heavens and the earth were made, before man fell or Angels rebelled, before the sons of God were formed in the morning of creation; yea, before there were Seraphim to veil their faces before Him and cry 'Holy', He existed without ministers, without attendants, without court and kingdom, without manifested glory, without anything but Himself; He His own Temple, His own infinite rest, His own supreme bliss, from eternity. O wonderful mystery! O the depth of His majesty! O deep things which the Spirit only knoweth! Wonderful and strange to creatures who grovel on this earth, as we, that He, the All-powerful, the All-wise, the All-good, the All-glorious, should for an eternity, for years without end, or rather, apart from time, which is but one of His creatures, that He should have dwelt without those through whom He might be powerful, in whom He might be wise, towards whom He might be good, by whom He might be glorified. O wonderful, that all His deep and infinite attributes should have been without manifestation! O wonderful thought! and withal, O thought comfortable to us worms of the earth, as often as we feel in ourselves and

see in others gifts which have no exercise, and powers which
are quiescent! He, the All-powerful God, rested from
eternity, and did not work; and yet, why *not* rest, wonderful
though it be, seeing He was so blessed in Himself? Why
should *He* seek external objects to know, to love, and to
commune with, who was all-sufficient in Himself? How
could He need fellows, as though He were a man, when He
was not solitary, but had ever with Him His Only-begotten
Word in whom He delighted, whom He loved ineffably,
and the Eternal Spirit, the very bond of love and peace,
dwelling in and dwelt in by Father and Son? Rather how
was it that He ever began to create, who had a Son without
beginning and without imperfection, whom He could love
with a perfect love? What exceeding exuberance of goodness was it that *He* should deign at length to surround
Himself with creation, who had need of nothing, and to
change His everlasting silence for the course of Providence
and the conflict of good and evil! I say nothing of the
apostasies against Him, the rebellions and blasphemies
which men and devils have committed. I say nothing of that
unutterable region of woe, the prison of the impenitent,
which is to last for eternity, coeval with Himself henceforth,
as if in rivalry of His blissful heaven. I say nothing of this,
for God cannot be touched with evil; and all the sins of
those reprobate souls cannot impair His everlasting felicity.
But, I ask, how was it that He who needed nothing, who
was all in all, who had infinite Equals in the Son and the
Spirit, who were One with Him, how was it that He created
His Saints, but from simple love of them from eternity?
Why should He make man in the Image of God, whose
Image already was the Son, All-perfect, All-exact, without
variableness, without defect, by a natural propriety and
unity of substance? And when man fell, why did He not

abandon or annihilate the whole race, and create others? Why did He go so far as to begin a fresh and more wonderful dispensation towards us, and, as He had wrought marvellously in Providence, work marvellously also in grace, even sending His Eternal Son to take on Him our fallen nature, and to purify and renew it by His union with it, but that, infinite as was His own blessedness, and the Son's perfection, and man's unprofitableness, yet, in His loving-kindness, He determined that unprofitable man should be a partaker of the Son's perfection and His own blessedness?

And thus it was that, as He had made man in the beginning, so also He redeemed him; and the history of this redemption we have been tracing for the last six months in our sacred Services. We have gone through in our memory the whole course of that Dispensation of active providences which God, in order to our redemption, has superinduced upon His eternal and infinite repose. First, we commemorated the approach of Christ, in the weeks of Advent; then His birth, of the Blessed Mary, after a miraculous conception, at Christmas; then His circumcision; His manifestation to the wise men; His baptism and beginning of miracles; His presentation in the Temple; His fasting and temptation in the wilderness, in Lent; His agony in the garden; His betrayal; His mocking and scourging; His cross and passion; His burial; His resurrection; His forty days, converse with His disciples after it; then His Ascension; and, lastly, the coming of the Holy Ghost in His stead to remain with the Church unto the end—unto the end of the world; for so long is the Almighty Comforter to remain with us. And thus, in commemorating the Spirit's gracious office during the past week, we were brought, in our series of representations, to the end of all things; and now what is left but to commemorate what will follow after

the end? The return of the everlasting reign of God, the
infinite peace and blissful perfection of the Father, the Son,
and the Holy Ghost, differing indeed from what it once was
by the fruits of creation and redemption, but not differing
in the supreme blessedness, the ineffable mutual love, the
abyss of holiness in which the Three Persons of the Eternal
Trinity dwell. He, then, is the subject of this day's celebra-
tion—the God of love, of holiness, of blessedness; in whose
presence is fullness of joy and pleasures for evermore; who
is what He ever was, and has brought us sinners to that
which He ever was. He did not bring into being peace and
love as part of His creation, but He was Himself peace and
love from eternity, and He blesses us by making us par-
takers of Himself, through the Son, by the Spirit, and He so
works in His temporal dispensations that He may bring us
to that which is eternal.

And hence, in Scripture, the promises of eternity and
security go together; for where time is not, there vicissitude
also is away. 'The Eternal God is thy refuge,' says Moses,
before his death, 'and underneath are the everlasting arms:
and He shall thrust out the enemy from before thee, and
shall say, Destroy them; Israel then shall dwell in safety
alone.' And again, 'Thou wilt keep him in perfect peace,
whose mind is stayed on Thee, because he trusteth in Thee.
Trust ye in the Lord for ever; for in the Lord Jehovah is
everlasting strength.' And again,

> Thus saith the High and Lofty One that inhabiteth eternity.
> . . . I dwell in the high and holy place, with him also that is of
> a contrite and humble spirit, to revive the spirit of the humble,
> and to revive the heart of the contrite ones. . . . I create the
> fruit of the lips; peace, peace to him that is afar off, and to
> him that is near.

And, in like manner, our Lord and Saviour is prophesied

of as being 'the *Everlasting* Father, the Prince of *peace*'. And again, speaking more especially of what He has done for us, 'The work of righteousness shall be *peace*; and the effect of righteousness, quietness, and *assurance for ever.*'[1]

As then we have for many weeks commemorated the economy by which righteousness was restored to us, which took place in time, so from this day forth do we bring before our minds the infinite perfections of Almighty God, and our hope hereafter of seeing and enjoying them. Hitherto we have celebrated His great works; henceforth we magnify Himself. Now, for twenty-five weeks we represent in figure what is to be hereafter. We enter into our rest, by entering in with Him who, having wrought and suffered, has opened the kingdom of heaven to all believers. For half a year we stand still, as if occupied solely in adoring Him, and, with the Seraphim in the text, crying, 'Holy, Holy, Holy,' continually. All God's providences, all God's dealings with us, all His judgments, mercies, warnings, deliverances, tend to peace and repose as their ultimate issue. All our troubles and pleasures here, all our anxieties, fears, doubts, difficulties, hopes, encouragements, afflictions, losses, attainments, tend this one way. After Christmas, Easter, and Whitsuntide, comes Trinity Sunday, and the weeks that follow; and in like manner, after our souls' anxious travail; after the birth of the Spirit; after trial and temptation; after sorrow and pain; after daily dyings to the world; after daily risings unto holiness; at length comes that 'rest which remaineth unto the people of God'. After the fever of life; after wearinesses and sicknesses; fightings and despondings; languor and fretfulness; struggling and failing, struggling and succeeding; after all the changes and chances of this troubled unhealthy state, at

[1] Deut. xxxiii. 27, 28; Isa. xxvi. 3, 4; lvii. 15. 19; ix. 6; xxxii. 17.

length comes death, at length the White Throne of God, at length the Beatific Vision. After restlessness comes rest, peace, joy—our eternal portion, if we be worthy—the sight of the Blessed Three, the Holy One; the Three that bear witness in heaven; in light unapproachable; in glory without spot or blemish; in power without 'variableness, or shadow of turning'. The Father God, the Son God, and the Holy Ghost God; the Father Lord, the Son Lord, and the Holy Ghost Lord; the Father uncreate, the Son uncreate, and the Holy Ghost uncreate; the Father incomprehensible, the Son incomprehensible, and the Holy Ghost incomprehensible. For there is one Person of the Father, another of the Son, and another of the Holy Ghost; and such as the Father is, such is the Son, and such is the Holy Ghost; and yet there are not three Gods, nor three Lords, nor three incomprehensibles, nor three uncreated; but one God, one Lord, one uncreated, and one incomprehensible.

Let us, then, use with thankfulness the subject of this day's Festival, and the Creed of St. Athanasius, as a means of peace, till it is given us, if we attain thereto, to see the face of God in heaven. What the Beatific Vision will then impart, the contemplation of revealed mysteries gives us as in a figure. The doctrine of the Blessed Trinity has been made the subject of especial contention among the professed followers of Christ. It has brought a sword upon earth, but it was intended to bring peace. And it does bring peace to those who humbly receive it in faith. Let us beg of God to bless it to us to its right uses, that it may not be an occasion of strife, but of worship; not of division, but of unity; not of jealousy, but of love. Let us devoutly approach Him of whom it speaks, with the confession of our lips and of our hearts. Let us look forward to the time when this world will have passed away and all its delusions; and when we, when every one born of woman, must either be in heaven or in hell. Let us desire to hide ourselves under the shadow of His wings. Let us beg Him to give us an understanding heart, and that love of Him which is the instinct of the new creature, and the breath of spiritual life. Let us pray Him to give us the spirit of obedience, of true dutifulness; an honest spirit, earnestly set to do His will, with no secret ends, no selfish designs of our own, no preferences of the creature to the Creator, but open, clear, conscientious, and loyal. So will He vouchsafe, as time goes on, to take up His abode in us; the Spirit of Truth, whom the world cannot receive, will dwell in us, and be in us, and Christ 'will love us, and will manifest Himself to us', and 'the Father will love us, and They will come unto us, and make Their abode with us'. And when at length the inevitable hour comes, we shall be able meekly to surrender our souls, our sinful yet redeemed souls, in much weakness and trembling, with much self-reproach and deep confession, yet in firm faith, and in cheerful hope, and in calm love, to God the Father, God the Son, God the Holy Ghost; the Blessed Three, the Holy One; Three Persons, One God; our Creator, our Redeemer, our Sanctifier, our Judge.*

*'Peace in Believing', *PPS*, VI, Sermon 25.